Introduction

Have you ever wondered how rare awakening is amongst the general population? I have. It is probably because suffering is so commonplace it is considered entirely normal, so normal that we don't even notice it.

When a person asks the question 'Why do I suffer?' it is a huge moment because from this point on it could be said that that person has awakened to the uncomfortable truth that there is someone here that is suffering. They have awakened because they see themselves as an object that suffers - in other words the absolute identification is over. In that one second of awareness the suffering is no longer theirs, it is the object, a 'me' that they identify as that suffers.

If you have picked this book up or purchased it online, I say well done to you, not because I wrote it, but because you already have some tiny inkling that there is suffering in your life and you might like to try and find a way out of it. However, if this is the case, it is the wrong book for you. I cannot help you suffer less. That task is better left to the self-help authors that deal with the many reasons and selves apparently suffering. But what I might be able to do is point the reader towards asking 'What' is it that thinks it suffers, what is the object that suffers? Because surely to answer the initial question on 'Why do I suffer?' we must ask where is the 'I'?

It can be said with all honesty that every book on spiritual enlightenment and awakening is old wine in a new bottle, but a féw of these bottles have blown away ideas that never again gained traction. I went off the rails and never got back on. Amongst these I should mention all the works of Wei Wu Wei but especially the book Posthumous Pieces. Another was the Chan master Huang Po and John Blofelds translation 'The Transmission of the Mind'

Most books about enlightenment have the same sales pitch. There is a 'you' here right now that can do some things, and if you do these things enough (this generally means for many years) these efforts will eventually bring about the desired state commonly known as enlightenment. Once you have reached this desired state you will no longer be subject to all the usual earthly annoyances - you might even survive physical death.

Along the way you must surrender to 'what is' even though 'what is' is impermanent. There is a job for life! Be more present, be kinder and compassionate to yourself and others especially those less fortunate than you, meditate a lot, become a vegan, maybe do yoga or follow a great master who has most likely been dead for centuries. If, however you do not reach enlightenment in this life you will have laid down some great foundations for the next life. Each spiritual experience you have is evidence that you are moving towards this prize, each misery a lesson that you are not learning what it is that you need to learn and must try harder. Does any of this sound familiar?

We set out on this apparent path believing from the out-set that we have the tools available to us that we can use to help us get what it is we want. Without question we have been conditioned that we own a mind without ever asking exactly where it is or for that matter how we use it, but apparently, we all suffer from owning one. We believe that we are troubled by our thoughts. We try and distance ourselves from our feelings and emotions based upon the premise that their causes are personal to us. We see the physical body as our temporary prison until at last at death we are freed from all of this. Life improves exponentially once we are dead and dependent upon how good we have been in this life will depend on what the next one is like.

One fundamental question that so few seekers ask themselves is 'What desires to be enlightened? What is it that is here right now reading these words, what is it that goes to retreats, watches teachers on You Tube and reads numerous books that no one else in their right mind would even consider picking up, let alone attempting to write? Of course, any answer to this question will only ever be another concept, but we must at least attempt to ask the question otherwise we are destined to float around in a trough of divine hypnosis happy clapping full of divine bliss.

From the very start you probably believed as I did that there was someone here alive today or at the very least could offer us advice or a prescribed path towards our desired aim. In the world of infinite information available at our fingertips we are used to getting what it is we want. Why not enlightenment as well? At some point in humanity's future the therapists trying to help people suffer less will outnumber those that need therapy .. we shall be living on planet Therapist!

When I wrote the Black Bird back in 2010 I wanted to walk the same fine line that so many authors on this subject attempt to walk. They offer you just enough information without really telling you the truth that you hope you are ready to hear. Is it that they don't know? Perhaps it is simply that their editors and agents will not allow them to tell you. Or perhaps it is out of compassion that they do not tell you the truth. Either way that is what I have avoided as much as possible in this book. I want to be explicitly honest with you from the start even at the risk of alienating you the reader. Another reason those authors might not expose the uncomfortable truth is there would be a mighty stampede of spiritual seekers running in the opposite direction taking with them their money and devotion. The book and author that tells you that there is no one here to get saved is not the kind of person most people want to listen to or read. In some way or another we are all invested in trying to save our own imaginary arses whether we are aware of that or not. Imagine for a moment that you no longer need to keep trying to save this fictitious entity from its apparent bondage. It might well be liberation from the idea that there is someone here that can achieve liberation for themselves.

Read on, see what you think..

What is seeking changes what is found.
What is found changes what seeks.
Self enquiry is a maze without an exit.

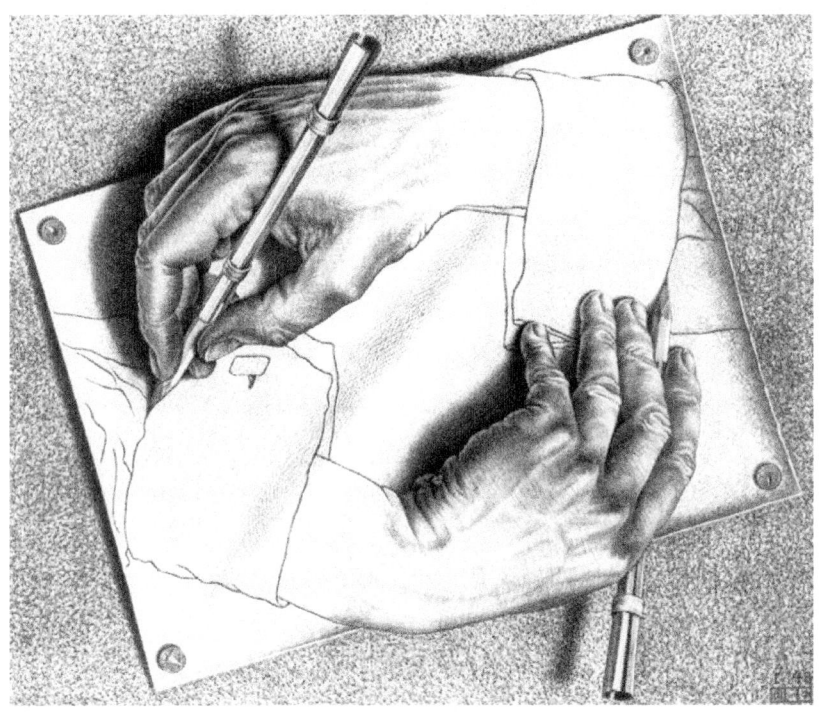

(MC Escher 1898 - 1972)

For Rupa my cat

The House of Cards

The Story of You

Chapter 1

Thought

'Thoughts arise and pass away. The proceeding no different from the succeeding. If the succeeding thought does not arise, the proceeding thought cuts itself off.'

Niutou Farong

In the tropics, there is a species of ant called the carpenter ant. That ant is unlucky enough to be infected by a fungus called *Ophiocordyceps unilateralis*. This rather unpleasant parasitic fungus physically changes the ant's behaviour by draining it of nutrients and hijacking its mind. Over the course of a week, it compels the ant to leave the safety of its nest and ascend to a nearby plant stem. It stops the ant at a height of 25 cm, a zone with precisely the right temperature and humidity for the fungus to grow. It forces the ant to permanently lock its mandibles around a leaf. Eventually, it sends a long stalk through the ant's head killing it, and the whole process repeats.

In a small town called Hawes North Yorkshire in the United Kingdom, there was young man called David. He was born and raised in a rather beautiful market town in what the British call God's own county. All his life he had always had trouble socializing and found it difficult to make friends; and in a small town where everyone knew each other, this felt akin to solitary confinement. David's awkward shyness was intensified by the agonizing observation that his classmates assessed his constantly troubled state as giving him an unacceptable air of weirdness. He was sure that the thoughts he was having were not the same as those other schoolchildren. He became so troubled by his internal narrative that he shared it with the young girl next door, someone he considered a friend. She promised him that it would be their secret. The next day at school, he was openly ridiculed by all those that now knew his thoughts…his friend had told everyone else at school. That evening, he crept out to the local beck, a name used for small streams in Yorkshire. He threw himself into the deepest pool he could find and drowned himself, thereby ending his short but rather anxious life.

Now we might think to ourselves that the carpenter ant did all of this against its will, but did the ant know it had a will in the first place, how would the ant know if it was its own choice or not? How would we tell the difference if it weren't for the fungus? Was David the young boy responsible for his thoughts? Were they in fact his thoughts? Did those thoughts only become his when he vocalized them? What would have happened if he had questioned those thoughts as "his" before driving himself to such drastic measures?

In this first chapter, I want to talk about thought and its effects on humanity, but also to you the spiritual seeker, and in what way this invisible energy affects that seeker. The similarities between the carpenter ant and the imaginary character called David is a rather perfect analogy for how humanity as a collective species has been hypnotized by thought. The primary reason for this is simple: We think that we think, that there is thinker here doing the thinking.

Because of the assumption that we are our thoughts and that we are responsible for the thinking, we hold each other accountable for the content of those thoughts; and therefore, all subsequent reactions. Our whole world system of law and government is based upon the premise that if a thought happens in my head it is mine. The main reason for this is simple; it is because the "you" that you think you are is also a thought, so it is a thought having thoughts! It gets far worse if the thought is spoken. If the thought is said aloud, it must be what you think and believe. To me this is very weird. It is the equivalent of holding the radio in the kitchen accountable for the music that is playing out of it. If the thoughts coming out of the persons mouth mirror our own perceived thoughts, we like this very much. However, if the thoughts challenge, contradict or even offend our own thoughts the person speaking is wrong and may need to be even imprisoned for them. This is the equivalent of throwing out the kitchen radio for playing Coldplay or even smashing it up it could get expensive, but understandable of course.

Close your eyes for one moment and visualize the planet Earth from space, or perhaps remember one of those NASA shots you may have seen of the earth. On this planet right now, there are 7.8 billion individuals all experiencing thoughts. The content of those thoughts shapes the apparent individual's behaviour, how one behaves, reacts, and moves through one's life. Then there are the very few who have stepped back sufficiently from thought to simply know it is just thought, nothing particularly special at all, just random energies. They are no longer slaves to the varied colours of these shifting spiraling energies of consciousness.

But for many humans on earth, thoughts behave very much like the ant fungus: They use their hosts --- us --- to proliferate. They even adapt their environments for further self-replication.

Thought behaves very much like a virus moving among the population using the host's DNA, or in this case the minds of humans, to replicate itself.

Think of perhaps religion as *thought*, because after all that is primarily all it is, a series of thoughts in the mind. Those thoughts actively change the behaviour of its host, they change the clothing, the language, its morals, what it consumes, which books it reads, its behavioural relationship with others around it; in every sense, it shapes the host's complete outlook on life and those it interacts with, just as the fungus did with the ant. It might even become more aggressive to those that do not share its beliefs, and in the worst-case scenario, it may even kill its host and others around it.

Under the influence of thought, people will seek out other people who share similar thought patterns and create echo chambers where there is a sense of safety for that organism. We naturally gravitate toward groups of people who share similar thoughts, what is a pollical rally but the collective outburst of mutual thoughts using humans as hosts. There is a sense of safety within that environment where thoughts congregate together...a spiritual retreat being no different from a church service.

Those that do not share their religious thoughts on life need to be coerced into believing what they do. This congregation of hosts under the influence of a collection of thoughts or beliefs works to the sole aim of spreading that message further and wider. These hosts build temples to worship that thought, which creates a more conducive environment for further thought self-replication, very much like the fungus adapting the ant's behaviour by making the ant climb to exactly 25 cm to promote its growth. In every sense of the word, the thought is using human hosts to build a temple in its own likeness. What you are seeing in all religious iconology is the physical manifestation of thought as form worshipping itself.

The thoughts will induce euphoria and states of bliss that give rise to addiction. This is especially effective when those thoughts are spoken aloud, danced, or physically expressed in some way. Thoughts of divinity and holiness light up those same areas of the human brain that cocaine and sex do, which might similarly account for the necessity of regular prayer and devotion. Hearing someone else verbalize what you think are your own personal thoughts has an immensely powerful effect on humans. This has been known by dictators, religious leaders, and politicians for time immemorial.

Over many generations, these thoughts become embedded into the population of a country and become the pillar stones of their culture. These cultures will go to great lengths in protecting their beliefs about themselves, their god, and their right to continue to believe in those thoughts. They will actively defend those against other cultures that do not share those values and beliefs...we call that war. On an individual basis, contradicting or even questioning these thoughts --- especially when there is a *god thought* involved -- can and often is fatal.

In some countries, merely questioning the mutually agreed truth of the collective thoughts of the population can lead to imprisonment and even the death penalty. Imagine that, if you can! To contradict the thoughts of someone else with other thoughts can literally be dangerous enough to lose your life. Sane? Does thought manipulate the organism's behaviour so that it does not put itself in harm by allowing itself to be silenced. It would seem a reasonable conclusion that if there are more humans with more weapons sharing a collective thought than those in the weaker position, that submissive behaviour would be one of reduced desire to vocalise it.

It seems that the ownership of a thought has an intimate relationship with the organism's right to survive, especially when it comes to the thought of god. The thought *god* seems to be beyond criticism or even question in some cultures. Imagine if I fought the police and authorities over my right to think of myself as a small horse called Derek; they would probably lock me up. But if the horse called Derek was a divine deeply holy horse, I might even get tax-free status and possibly even the finances to build a few churches in addition.

People under the influence of deeply entrenched belief systems usually pass it on to their children. Over many generations, we might even be able to see physical evidence of those thought patterns in the body, although this is hotly debated, as it implies that thought can literally affect the host's DNA.

Thoughts use their hosts in often extremely violent ways. How many of us defend thoughts that we have daily, thoughts we personally own? We identify with thought so thoroughly that those thoughts *need* defending; especially if someone contradicts them; or maybe it is the thought itself using us to defend itself against other contradictory thoughts. Perhaps it is part of the thought's survival mechanism, to attack other contradictory memes using humans as their hosts.

Thought uses humanity to create collective ideologies, political structures, nation-state identities, race, gender. Thought can energize whole nation-states into mass slaughter against other nation-states that do not share in those thoughts. Thought does not see other fellow humans, it only sees opposites, to convince that it is right and they are wrong. Whilst humans are addicted to thought, there will never be any real union of mind.

Think about what most wars and all physical, emotional violence comes down to: is it not simply two contradictory thoughts using humans to fight it out?

Imagine if, in that singular moment, both arguing humans became aware that they were being used by thoughts, that neither of them identified with those thoughts as true or false, that they were simply nothing more than transient energies. Would I take your life because a different thought happened in your mind? I think what you are thinking is wrong; thus, at first, I am going to try and convince you that you are wrong. If that does not work, I will raise my voice so what I think increases in power. Then finally, when all that fails I will physically harm you, thereby proving to you that my thoughts were right all along.

So, are we responsible for thoughts?

If you sit quietly for a few moments, perhaps just listening to your immediate environment, thoughts will naturally pop up into the conscious mind, probably thoughts about those things you can hear or see. Is there a choice before the thought happens as to how quickly or slowly that thought will arrive? Is there a choice about the content of that thought, the subject matter? At which point do we take ownership of that thought -- or is it instantaneous? For most people, these questions simply do not arise. They are so utterly unconditionally identified with thought that it is their whole identity and existence.

But if the practice of scrutinising our thoughts is carried out a few times, it soon becomes clear that is not the case; there is no one here doing the thinking, rather the thinking is just something that is happening. Ask yourself, why would you defend a thought just because it happens to arise in your mind? Don't you have a will of your own?

Many thoughts go unjudged, unnoticed even. We do not often make the obvious link between our actions and the thoughts behind them, we simply find ourselves on autopilot, doing the bidding of thought without even questioning it, monkey think--monkey do. That is, until someone asks us why we did what we did. Why did the ant climb the branch and bite onto the stalk?

Over time, certain thoughts become repetitive; and these repetitive thoughts become beliefs about things.

If these thoughts are backed up with physical evidence -- for instance, in childhood when an adult points at a fruit and says "orange" and repeats that again and again: "orange, orange" -- the child will be permanently conditioned to think of all fruits of that colour as an orange and as tasting like an orange. As we mature and become adults, it gets increasingly difficult for that to change. As adults, we like to hold onto what we know as sole truth, the only truth there is. Contrary evidence is mostly ignored. Confirmation bias is how we maintain a sense of safety in our lives.

People generally feel they are free to think what they want from moment to moment, never realising that they have been utterly brainwashed by the media, culture, and television. Today, social media bombards the minds of the young with advertising, political agendas, news-driven agendas, religious beliefs, and so forth, such that it is hardly surprising we have such a massive increase in self-harming and suicide in young people. Their minds are never quiet. But here is a weird idea for you. If we blame those people utilizing the media to their own advantage for whatever reason, are we not missing the whole point of this chapter? Is it not the thoughts themselves that have hypnotized those people telling us what to think?

Who is guilty or innocent here if the whole human race is under the spell of thinking their thoughts are their own?

We think of ourselves as the user of thought much like we use a mobile phone, that we employ some mechanism to bring about thought like pressing the keys on a phone. But when this apparent process is scrutinized even for a few seconds, it becomes blatantly clear that this is not the case. There is no user of thought, rather there is just thought happening as a function of life. You cannot tell me how you think, you cannot even prove to me you actually have thoughts, let alone thoughts that are unique to you.

Our language is strewn with such sentences as these:

"You need to think carefully about that."

"Do you have any thoughts on the subject?"

"My thoughts are my own."

"She straightened her hair and collected her thoughts."

I particularly like this last one, mostly because she had hair to straighten.

So, let us get down to the nuts and bolts of this. Thought happens, it gives rise to the illusion of a thinker, a *me*. I am the thinker of thoughts; therefore, I am those thoughts. It really is that basic.

So, can we stop being a host to thoughts and their seemingly random outputs? What would that look like to us. Well first, we must start to become aware of our own habitual thought patterns. It is a good place to start.

Is, for instance, a thought true or false, right or wrong? And who gets to decide that? Surely, it requires another thought to judge that thought. It becomes an incessant tirade of successive

thoughts, each chasing the previous one. This can give rise to the illusion that "you" are the victim of thoughts; is this really possible?

It begs the question: "Who is the victim of thoughts"? Who is it being plagued by thoughts? Let me give you a common example of a typical internal narrative. Here is one familiar example of

someone talking to oneself as if it is two people; the one is not aware that it's merely two thoughts chatting away to each other:

"So, what do I feel like doing today?"

"God, I am tired, I didn't sleep that well last night, probably drank too much wine, I really should cut down on how many glasses I have."

"Who is that in the bathroom??" Oh my god, he takes forever in there and I really need to get to work."

"I wonder if he really loves me, we have been together a couple of years now."

"Oh, why are you worrying about that, you are still quite a catch, and besides, Simon in the office has taken a bit of interest recently so at least someone is there if it all goes wrong with this one."

"You know it always does, it is only a matter of time, do not think that, remember you promised yourself you would try harder in this one." "Oh, he is out of the bathroom, about bloody time."

When this type of thought is happening inside your mind, who exactly are you talking to. Is that thought you? If so, then who is talking to whom? Isn't it two thoughts conversing? Could it be that you are merely an innocent bystander, that our lives are a testimony to mistaken identity?

As the thinker of thoughts, you are under the illusion that you can control them, in order to only have pleasant thoughts. But isn't all that effort always in hindsight? Once the thought has already happened, sounds like a great deal of effort to me, constantly censoring and attempting to control thoughts. But if we do not control thoughts, the thoughts will run riot, and once again, we are back to the imaginary victim suffering under the tyranny of unpleasant thoughts.

Thoughts are not a problem if you know that they are simply an energetic description of events that have already happened. A thought is very much like a child's drawing of a giraffe on the kitchen fridge, a conceptual overlay, never the actual thing itself.

The thought *water* cannot quench your thirst or make a good cup of tea. If the thought *water* cannot quench your thirst or make a cup of tea, then how accurate is that thought that you think you are no good or that you are or are not a hot sex god or goddess?

In fact, is there a single thing that you think is true or false that makes up your own entire matrix of existence -- anything at all other than a description? God how scary is that? Because if that is true, who has been doing all the doing and running your massively successful life? Or who is it that is a complete and utter failure.

So, can we function without the incessant narrative of this fictitious entity created through thinking?

In meditation, it is a common practice simply to not engage with thought at all. Thought happens; like a barking dog, it attempts to get the sitter's attention. If the sitter spends sufficient time ignoring habitual thought patterns, the thoughts themselves lose momentum and become a whole lot less frequent. Please take my word for this, as this has happened to me. Yes, I am aware of the paradoxical nature of that last sentence.

But here is the essential piece of information. You must **ignore ALL** thoughts, not just the ones that make you out to be a sad lonely loser or too fat, but the ones you like, as well. The ones that tell you that you are one bloody hot babe or mister stud with the birds. Attaching self-worth to thoughts you enjoy only creates the opposite thoughts you do not enjoy...it is still a fictious entity based on thought.

What happens when thoughts cease altogether? This can feel very much like being in a circus highwire act without a safety net, mostly because without identifying with thought there is no self for a frame of reference. If you think about it for moment, don't you self-reference with yourself in your head all day? *Who is talking to whom?*

If there is no "I" claiming that it is the one in charge doing all the doing, then how is any of this happening. Is it enough to just say, "Oh, it is happening"? The question I hear most from seekers is this: "If I am not in charge doing the doing, then things won't get done, my life will unravel, who's going to do all the stuff that needs doing?" And my answer is exactly the same each time: "You assume you have been the one doing it up until now, so if you haven't, then what actually is going to change?" Pretty much nothing except everything at the exact same time.

So, what is life like without the need for constant self-referencing? As strange as this might sound, we already do it a lot of the time. Surely, you can make a cup of tea or coffee without the incessant need for thought to tell you the next action to take! Do you need a thought to know what gear to change in the car when you are driving? Well, if you can agree with that, then try to expand that idea outward into your daily life, outward into every tiny detail of your day-to-day movements and actions. It really is not that scary, it is what is called in Zen *spontaneous functioning* or Wei Wu Wei, *doing without doing*. As in, life is a permanent series of catching falling objects from the kitchen cupboard, then congratulating yourself for doing something you didn't actually decide to do.

Looking or seeing life without the lens of conceptualising everything, we really do only then start to see the world as it is. We look at a tree and we quite literally have no idea what it is, we might look at a partner, friend, or lover and not actually know who they are. This might sound a little weird, but without that constant overlay of the shared history made up of thoughts, true emotional intimacy might arise. We listen, we see, just in that moment, without needing anything to be about a *me* or an *us*.

Leading onto the next chapter --- "The sense of self" --- I want to point out that the very foundational stones of the entity we think ourselves to be, complete with free will and freedom to do what we please, are made up of and created by the endless identification with thought. It is not of course our entire house of cards but it is a major aspect, without doubt.

Well, if you have gotten this far without falling off your perch, please carry on.

Chapter 2

The self

'There is nobody and nothing to be aware of Awareness. I cannot be aware of myself, for I know no self of which I could be aware.'

Wei Wu Wei

Before I start to write about this phenomenon I call the self, I want to point out to you that I am using a lowercase letter *s* when I describe the *self* in this and subsequent chapters unless otherwise stated. In spiritual books of this ilk, the self with a lowercase *s* is not the *Self* with an uppercase letter *S*. Self and self are not interchangeable. They are entirely distinct and different in their meaning.

The reason for clarifying this at the start is especially important to those of you who have any experience with Advaita or the Indian/Hindu teachings. Those texts use an uppercase *S* to make a distinction between the *sense of self* and *the Self*. As the Self with an uppercase *S* is not mentioned here, I doubt it will cause any problems. Problems arise when these two words are not defined with such statements as "All there is is Self" with a lowercase *s* in midsentence. Does this mean all there is is me or is there another type of *me* I have no knowledge of yet, a me with a higher purpose! Often there is a great deal of confusion when reading spiritual texts, as it is not always obvious whether the author is pointing to the eternal concept using a capital letter or individual ownership of something using a lowercase letter.

I also want to avoid onion peeling the sense of self from one individual to another; this is more in the realm of psychology and leads down a path towards specifics of personality. Let us just say we all have the same characteristics that differ in degrees to a greater or lesser extent.

You might not find many books discussing the sense of self and enlightenment together. Books that talk about the sense of self are mostly about improving upon such an idea as the self: a "self-help" book, of which there are millions. This is not one of those, by the way. The very notion of self-help is somewhat preposterous, as it would require a self to take up two separate spaces -- one *here* helping another self over *there*, both of which are apparently *you*!

The sense of self is the lens to the external world around us; and like a kaleidoscope, it colours every experience, it is the reference point that filters the external information through which we navigate life. It is also how we interact with fellow humans. For most people, it is all there is --- that is, identification as self --- not as "having" a self. So, to the spiritual seeker, it is utterly essential to delve deeply into those colours that make up this ever-shifting fractal of the apparent experiencer and how it shapes that seeking process.

To discuss the self, though, we must first objectify it --- that is, make it an object from the outset. Most of the time, we do not think about ourselves from an objective standpoint because we are entirely identified as a self. The self only really comes into view when we talk about ourselves and others in the second person. For instance, if we are asked about some individual, we describe who that is based upon our memories and interactions with this individual.

If, for instance, we have been to a job interview, we might be asked to describe ourselves. To do this, we objectify ourselves, we think of ourselves as an object in the mind much the same way we might do with any object when we recall it. In a job interview, we then proceed to describe ourselves as a collection of positive and negative attributes.

In this chapter, I hope to convince the spiritual seeker how important the self is. It has been much maligned by spiritual teachers and even dismissed as not existing at all. Dismiss the self at your own risk; because to reach the goal of awakening, it is not only our view of that process, it is through that self that any awakening is experienced.

The spiritual seeker is primarily obsessed with answering what one considers major questions. Those might be, "Why do I suffer?" and "How can I reduce my suffering?"

Let us discuss suffering first, before we move on with more talk of the self, as these two — suffering and the self --- have an intimate relationship.

In order to know that we are suffering, there must be some expansion or what appears to be an evolution of a kind within our awareness; we must move from the full immersion within our habitual stories to a more mindful experience of those storylines, to literally become aware of suffering in order to say, "I am suffering." This is no mean feat. The seedling of awakening is the knowledge that I am suffering in the first place. I have had people say to me, "What do you mean I am suffering? No I'm not."

Why am I saying that it is so difficult to answer that question? It is simply because suffering is our mainstay experience and identity. It is so commonplace, in fact, that you may need to stop reading this and become aware of your suffering — again, no easy feat. When one's suffering has been denied --- and I have, in response, gone on to describe one's clear and constant experience of suffering --- it is often met with quite aggressive protectionism, as if I am hurling a personal attack on this individual. The sense of self has a unique ability towards confirmation bias. That is, that whatever happens to the individual, it always manages to rejuggle those events in such a way that it makes itself the centre of attention. It can be quite ruthless in moving the bits and pieces of the jigsaw to support the necessary narratives that it feels will protect the individual. "It is only other people that suffer, not me! I am fine."

To conclude that "I" am suffering is a determination about which you may congratulate yourself --- but no need to go full Oscar --- no need to milk it to death, simply recognize that there is a constant state of dissatisfaction in your life and you are curious as to the root of that.

I will say I have concluded over the years that people really do enjoy suffering. As glib as that sounds, suffering has one great benefit to the sense of self --- it renders this self more important than other selves. Suffering is familiar, comforting, and extremely addictive. It is how we come to know that we exist, so much so that it would seem people are wired to seek out new and inventive ways to create more suffering for themselves. If they are suffering, they have an interesting personality.

The sense of self actively seeks out storylines that create mayhem and drama, thereby establishing itself as the lead actor or actress in its own movie, marketed as such to all other selves; and likewise, these other selves are themselves compelled to enter the competition for more attention. We have all noticed that the characters in a TV soap opera always bring it back to blaming themselves: It is my suffering and everything is my fault; I did this, so I need to sort it out. That is the vocalized version of the self. It is a deeply unhealthy cycle, but it is so common that those who no longer participate in this are themselves considered abnormal, out of touch, and a bit vague in character and personality, even a little dismissive of the endless diatribe of problems that some people are desperate to air on a continuous basis.

Most people on this planet are entirely oblivious to their own suffering, let alone the suffering they inflict on others. I would go so far as to say that your own suffering is mirrored in those closest to you. When you find yourself trying to help reduce someone else's suffering, you are in fact making the first attempts to reduce your own. "What" is suffering turns out be a far more evolved question than "who" is it that suffers. "Who is suffering?" assumes by definition that suffering is personal to you the individual; and so the answer to that question will always logically include a *you* at the centre of that answer.

If a person is asked the question "Who is suffering," the sensible answer will always be, "*I* am suffering." But when we close our own personal playbook just for a moment and ask instead, "*What* is suffering?" it is far easier to stand back and take a deeper look at the suffering itself — the *what*, not the *who*.

When the seeker first begins to think of oneself as a sufferer, it is usually about the Big Stuff: Perhaps it is a health issue, a lack of material means, drug addiction, a dysfunctional relationship, a crappy job. Take your pick --- there are as many versions of suffering as there are the minutiae of characteristics within this thing I am calling the self. Suffering can also be exquisitely subtle; it does not have to include such extremes as homelessness or an emotionally insensitive partner. It can be not getting your coffee made correctly because your favourite barista has been fired for fraternizing with the boss behind the tills.

Suffering is psychologically accumulative, too. In a single day, a person will collect an entire book of trigger points from unsatisfactory outcomes, build a case that one is suffering far worse than anyone else, then meet up with friends in the evening and replay the game reel, energizing those events into one big drama. This can and does happen over a lifetime until, layer by layer, we are crushed by our own apparent history.

However: sometimes, something inside us snaps, and we literally think we cannot or will not go on like this.

The level of suffering in the individual is in direct relationship with how much we identify ourselves as a separate, autonomous individual with free will, making events happen in our lives through our personal efforts. Think about how much energy and effort is expended on a daily level as we try to achieve a level of satisfaction or indeed safety for this self. It utterly consumes both the individual and humanity as a whole. The world and particularly mainstream media are constantly telling us we are unsafe, that we are in danger; but from minute to minute, this is simply not the case.

Once again, I want to set a gentle reminder here that the sense of self colours the view we have of the world. Although we could so easily get into semantics here, the nuances of what makes a *me* as opposed to a *you*, that is not my intent here; your experience is yours, mine is mine. Comparing selves is a never-ending cycle of competitive suffering. In the United Kingdom, this is a soap opera called *EastEnder*s; in the States, it's *Housewives* of [fill in the blanks] *County*.

I need to add that it is impossible to find a consummate answer to the question of the self, it is like the M.C. Escher drawing of the hand sketching the other hand that is sketching the other hand, always and forever changing! Or perhaps if that metaphor does not work, it is like a set of Russian dolls, an infinite fractal of ever-decreasing descriptions without a satisfactory conclusion. This is why the Buddha used the following teaching so as to reduce the amount of seeking time people spent hunting out answers to this riddle.

'"Was I in the past? Shall I be in the future? Am I? Am I not? What am I? ...'

As he attends inappropriately in this way, one of six kinds of view arises in him:

'I have a self...'

'I have no self...'

'It is precisely by means of self that I perceive self...'

'It is precisely by means of self that I perceive not-self...'

'It is precisely by means of not-self that I perceive self...'

'This very self of mine ... is the self of mine that is constant...'

This is called a thicket of views, a wilderness of views, a contortion of views, a writhing of views, a fetter of views. Bound by a fetter of views, the uninstructed ... is not freed, I tell you, from suffering & stress."

My personal history and sense of self, which is very much intact, will of course colour what I write here for you, but I am going to give it a damn good go. To attempt to describe the self with absolute certainty would be as crazy as comparing two hamburgers, one in New York and another one in London, and proclaiming that if the Londoner hamburger does not taste or look like the one in New York, then it is not a hamburger, it is something else.

But we can point to enough hamburgers to get a rough guide to the essential nature, the suchness, of "hamburger." Because the nature of the sense of self is impermanent, nailing it down as an exact object is somewhat difficult, but we can describe it. We can say enough about it to step aside from it and point to it and say, "That is the self."

As I have previously stated, the only way to talk about the sense of self is to objectify it. Like a scientist, stand back and peel away a few layers. To do this, I have compared it with something else, analogized it: I want to offer up the image of a mirage as my analogy because I think this works especially well.

According to Google, a mirage is an optical illusion caused by atmospheric conditions, especially the appearance of a sheet of water in a desert or on a hot road caused by the refraction of light from the sky by heated air. I know some people who become more like hot air when they have had a few drinks and even some folks that can do impersonations of being droplets (but never a lake).

The sense of self is not literally a mirage, but it does share more in common with a mirage than you might first think. For instance, a mirage is an illusion --- that is, it has no independent existence in and of itself; it is inseparable from its immediate environment. If a person dying of thirst in the desert is staggering towards a mirage where the illusion of cool water will save his or her life and you pop up and say, "That doesn't really exist," it is doubtful they will give you much attention.

However, if you say to that poor person, "That there is some right lovely cool fresh thirst-quenching water," that is equally untrue.

You might have come across many spiritual teachers that say there *is no* such thing as the sense of self. Those teachers are the ones saying to the dying person in the desert that there is no mirage. The teachers saying there *is* a sense of self are taking up an equally inaccurate view: the sense of self is both an illusion and not an illusion, simultaneously. It has sufficient existence to be completely believable, enough to keep a whole planet preoccupied with maintaining that illusion; yet it has no independent existence.

Those of you who have spent any time in Non-Duality circles on social media or otherwise will have found this out to your cost; arguing the point that there definitely is not a sense of self only proves the opposite. In the ancient teachings of Chan and Zen, teachers simply whacked their student with a stick or pulled their nose harshly and asked, "So who's feeling the pain and anger?" To say something does not exist is to say it did exist and now does not exist. This is a quite common error, especially in Neo-Advaita circles (New-Neo).

The mirage, like the self, not only has an intimate relationship with its immediate environment but is entirely dependent upon the conditions for its existence. Both the mirage and the sense of self share this similarity.

Are you, for instance, the same self in the office with your boss floating about as that person who pulls up into the driveway after work and greets one's partner, children, family pet? Are you the exact same person as the one with an old friend as you are with the shop assistant in your local supermarket? How do you feel when an old friend that has known you in your misspent youth comes to stay with you and your partner (who has never met the friend before)? Would you feel vulnerable? Does the sense of self try to control that environment in order to avoid having hidden aspects of its past revealed?

The immediate environment not only gives rise to the sense of self. I would go as far as to say it is inseparable from its immediate surroundings. The question must be asked, "How much control is there over those conditions outside us that give rise to the variations in this self?" Sure, we can decide to not invite our embarrassing family members to the wedding or Christmas because we don't like that version of the self; but what about those events that happen spontaneously, the more subtle energies happening moment to moment; how much control do we really ever have over those? How much time is spent trying to control those?

It is true that we prefer ourselves when we are with some people and not so much with others. We return to the same restaurants and holiday destinations because we have fond memories of how we felt there. Maybe we felt that we could express ourselves more freely and fully in that place with that group of people. We might even return to a place to rekindle some self that we found there; we might say, "Ah yes, I felt I could really be myself (in that place or with that person)."

It is this object with mirage-like qualities that has no independent existence of its own that must in some way be satisfied by events that it sets out to achieve for itself. This can be the greatest source of suffering! Can the sense of self ever truly be satisfied? How does what is impermanent find completion? Most of the world's population has no idea that the self exists, simply because their identification with it is absolute, there is no separation: I am my name, my job, a husband, a brother, a bank manager, gay, straight, white or black, Jewish, Muslim, or Buddhist. *I am those things, this is what I am*, and because this is me I need to defend it with the utmost vehemence.

More and more now as I write in 2020, the unconscious desire to identify with minority labels seems to be becoming part of the human survival strategy. I actually think that the greater the population of humanity, the worse this will get. The desire to be heard above the crowd is all about being noticed, much as it's done by the youngest sibling in a large family unit. But to the spiritual seeker, a transient label is not enough, it is an unsatisfactory conclusion to what am I because those very identities, those labels, have been the primary cause of my suffering. Sometimes hefty divine identification with something such as "I am" or the "Self" might be sufficient --- a more spiritual story than those other selves is a quite common theme in the world of seeking...this merely making the sense of self more divine than another's, and you can't get a more divine self than an enlightened self.

The sense of self does not just exist on its own, even when it is in a solitary environment such as a Buddhist cave dwelling. It has continuous interaction with other selves within its own world. In spiritual circles, this will most commonly be called, "The Story" or "My Story." Of course, even outside seeking circles, every individual has a story.

The story of the self gives rise to the illusion of linear time, that is, it came into existence at some point in the past, a birthdate, then developed over time until right now, the now being a thing we conceptualise and call the present. The sense of self that you consider yourself to be right now thinks or rather believes that if it could be more present it would make its life more peaceful, but the mere act of trying only deepens the illusion of time, or rather the movement in and out of this object called the present.

When we go to sleep at night, that is myself falling asleep; when we awake in the morning, there I am too --- as if the pause button on a tape recording has been pressed and we are somehow magically reborn. In truth the self is born and dies each time a thought of ourselves is identified with, how many times a day is that?

The story of a self is the accumulated events that have happened to it. It got born, it was a child, summers seemed longer, it went to school, it did exams, it left school, had a great time at college, started work, became successful, got married, had children, became a parent, got divorced, was single again, remarried, got divorced again, drank too much, slept on a park bench, and died alone in the snow on Christmas day. All remarkably interesting and deeply important to the person that is experiencing it. And of course, there are degrees of success for the self as well. Went to school, got a degree, became a surveyor, owned my own company, sold it, retired at 45 as a millionaire, married woman half my age, got divorced, became an alcoholic, and now sleep in my brother's spare room. Sorry, I could not help myself, but you get the picture.

Through that period of a lifetime, the self appears to go through an infinite number of changes. It reminds me of those fractal animations you can find on YouTube, iridescent colours and shapes, repeating and evolving over a lifetime. Those changes joined up together appear as one long story, because that is how we have evolved to perceive time. But what if I suggested to you that although those changes appear to us as evolution of the self --- as if the self develops, learns even --- like the fractal, absolutely nothing at all has happened. Like watching a merry-go-round repeatedly over a lengthy period, it only appears to change in a lifetime due to the illusion of time. That is the space between apparent events.

What if those events were just random and the mind has evolved to join them together to create the illusion of continuity --- continuity we call our life or our story?

Our story is quite literally the most important aspect of our lives. When we speak about ourselves, we are recalling events that have happened to us, not to anyone else, but to ourselves. The sense of self is often all we have in order to express our intimate relationship with ourselves, each other, and the world; without a story, there literally is no one here. In fact, people are often described as interesting characters based entirely upon their story. We judge each other through our stories. Our worth to ourselves is often based upon how we interpret the past, how we might leave out bits we do not like --- there is a great tendency for self-promotion within the insular space of our own personal universe. Other people's stories might be how we define these people as interesting and perhaps intend to keep them around for our own entertainment.

Those other selves within our lives playing the co-stars in our story, are they not just as impermanent and fictitious as we ourselves are, do they not have mirage-like qualities as well? That is quite a statement to get your head around, isn't it?

Who do I really love and hate, in what way does this self decide who gets its attention and who does not? It can get rather scary when we really start to look deeply into this mental landscape of our own personal universes, because we might start to wonder what we can define as real and unreal.

So, if the sense of self is an object in the mind, one that we can describe, one that we recall, does that mean we are remembering ourselves? When we are asked about another person, we are remembering them; how is that different from the character we think we are?

If this is the case, how accurate is that memory of ourselves, what we said, what we did last week, last month, 5 or 10 years ago? Have you noticed that when you speak about yourself to people, sometimes it does not quite add up? That we embellish certain areas of our personality in order to impress, excite, or even turn on the listener. How many times have you heard yourself actively bullshitting at a job interview---or worse still, on a first date---isn't there a little Patrick Bateman in all of us.

In spiritual circles, you might often hear a spiritual seeker say, "I am not my story." What does that mean?

It is as if they have dismissed their entire experience up to that point as having less than any part in their lives, leaving off their back-catalogue of exchanges, the infinite variety of desires that led them to this point, as insignificant. It is disingenuous to disregard the self, to declare it has no active part or any essential role in the seeking process; without the sense of self, there would be no seeking. No self, no suffering, no seeking.

Within the story of the sense of self, there will naturally be other characters. The spiritual teacher is perhaps the most important of these because he or she will actively help the sense of self, the apparent individual, to awaken.

The most important characteristic of the teacher to the self is that the self must believe --- unconditionally --- that the teacher is an awakened individual; otherwise, what is the point? The seeker does not go to a retreat to listen to Bill the dustman; it goes and spends lots of money at a retreat in Portugal and sits at the feet of the teacher. Often that teacher will have a photograph of his or her teacher, a kind of picture book lineage to add credence to his or her own story of awakening, a certification of authenticity.

But a spiritual teacher will never say he or she is awakened. The onus is on the seeker to maintain the belief that this person has something you do not have and that you must therefore hold onto the illusion that you too can one day get it as well. As long as this desire from the sense of self insists that awakening is available to it, this relationship will continue, and often for years and to great expense as well.

So, the spiritually awakened teacher is as much a part of the story of the self as the self is to itself, is it not? A bit like the Russian dolls I mentioned earlier.

We might not like to admit this to ourselves, but let us be honest. The spiritual teacher is just as much a part of the story of the self as finding the perfect partner might be, or perhaps buying a great house with sea views.

But mirages are limited by the environment. If I take further license with my analogy here, the self appears to have an infinite variety of colours, yet it is actually made up of a "finite" number of colours: Mix them up in any quantity or quality you can imagine and you can create all of the art seen across the history of humanity, everything that was ever painted or drawn or thought. But all those wonderful creations were still only five primary colours. We cannot step outside that limitation set by the nature of the self just as the mirage is inescapably restricted by the sun's spectrum. The mirage is the story of me and my life and is always inclusive of all and every aspect of the story.

What does this say about suffering and the self's desire to reduce that? What does this say about liberation from that suffering? What does this ultimately mean for the seeker in the search for a way out of one's suffering by attaining this Great Awakening. Could it be as simple as saying that awakening is simply another story for the sense of self? This very liberation is the realisation itself --- that there is no thing here that can be liberated for the simple reason that there was never any object that was bound.

So, if the sense of self has no independent existence other than as an imagined object, can it bring about its own salvation, its eternal absolution? Is it possible for this object do anything at all?

What is essential to understand, at least intellectually, is that within the story of the self, anything is possible; all the colours of the mirage are shifting and moving around. Therefore, yes --- the self can indeed be liberated, but only ever within the story of itself. The greatest belief of all is that there is someone here that can achieve awakening, that this self can follow a path to that aim. It is the eternal optimism of the self, to "reach Nirvana," to "see Heaven," "to be saved."

The story will, of course, continue "post-realisation": that there was no one here to be liberated simply because the story is this as well. The sense of self will keep shifting and changing because that is its nature. The self is just as much a part of the human experience as is breathing. Those that say there is no self, and the story has stopped, have created a nonstory --- a story about not having a story! The "I don't have a story" is also a story, so there is no escaping this fictious entity living rent-free as every human on earth. The big difference is so minor, yet utterly impossible to really talk about because as soon as you talk about it, it is the past, and that is another story. We can but only objectify this because there is and there is not this, simultaneously.

So, don't bother trying to live without a self or a story, it is enough to know it is a story. It is the mirage, incredibly mind-blowing, often entertaining, sometimes damn-right tragic, and forever leading itself around and around in a never-ending story of being saved from its own imaginings.

<u>Chapter 3</u>

The Mind

'The arising and the elimination of illusions are both illusory. Illusion is not something rooted in reality: it exists because of dualistic thinking. If you will only cease to indulge in opposed concepts such as 'ordinary' and 'enlightened' illusion will cease of itself'

Huang Po

For this chapter, I would like to ask you to carry out two small experiments of your own right where you are sitting or standing at this moment. To do this, you may need to open a window or at the very least become acutely aware of one specific noise that you can hear and one that you enjoy. It does not have to be of any particular quality, but it may make the experiment easier if it is the loudest sound you can hear.

Listen very carefully. Really concentrate on the sound you have chosen; try to pinpoint one sound out of the cacophony if you are in a city. If it is too difficult to do this right now, try it later when there is not a wall of noise.

There are two questions I want to ask you.

The first question is this: What mechanism do you directly employ to hear that sound?

The reason I ask you, the reader, what mechanism you employ to hear an object is that it points to the truth that no one at all uses any mechanism to hear. You do not adjust the physical ear on the side of your head in any way, you do not alter the volume by manipulating the tympanum or fiddle with the hammer or anvil, or for that matter the stirrup. There is a vast chain of events all entirely out of our doing that brings about the act of hearing that sound. In every sense of the word, *you are not needed*.

Is it such a massive stretch of the mind to say that hearing is simply happening? Even when there are no sounds to hear, hearing is still happening. If we then add the other senses to this, such as seeing, touching, tasting, and smelling, who is doing any of that also? Those are literally the matrices of reality as we know it. We can easily begin to see that reality, whatever that means, has absolutely nothing at all to do with any you; you have no say in these data being received, how the information is translated, what the result of that process may be...yet there is an "I" continuously laying claim to the doing of that.

The second question is this: Is that sound inside or outside your mind? This is somewhat trickier to explain.

We have been conditioned to believe that we have a mind of our own, a private sanctuary that is somewhere between our ears and inside the skull. No one has ever seen the mind or has pointed to such a thing as "my mind," but our language is riddled with evidence that such an object as mind exists.

"Make your mind up, will you!"

Exactly how does one go about making a mind up? At the risk of repeating myself, what physical mechanism do you use to make a mind up. Is it like me pressing the keys on my mobile phone, then clicking Send? Could it be that part of the process when decisions, choices, and preferences are taken includes the proclamation of personal agency by the illusory sense of self?

For there to be a "me" here to make up "a mind," that *me* would need to be separate from that object called a mind, much like you use a mobile phone. If that "I" laying claim to this process *is* the process, how can it be separate from it? It cannot.

There clearly is not a "you" tapping away at the synapses controlling the decision-making process like the Wizard of Oz or the Numskulls in the Beano comic. Is this tantamount to saying that you do not exist? Not quite. It's only asking the reader — just like the previous two chapters --- where exactly does this *you* exist? At which juncture of that infinitely long process is a *you* needed for it all to happen, if at all.

The inevitable consequence there possibly being no *you* here physically utilising an object called the mind (let alone owning such a thing) is rather startling, maybe even unpleasant. But also perhaps hugely liberating as well. Who exactly has made those life decisions that you considered unwise or left you emotionally messed up, traumatised even? Is not everyone entirely innocent of every choice they appeared to have made? How many times did Jesus or the Buddha point this out? Quite a few times, on my reckoning.

In the Diamond Sutra alone, the Buddha points out no less than 109 times that there is no self doing the doing. Jesus' teachings are somewhat more subtle and polluted by time; and those who heeded those pointers were driven by their own personal agendas. Maybe Psalm 39:5-6: "Indeed every living man is no more than a puff of wind, no more than a shadow. All he does is for nothing."

Because our habit as humans is to objectify everything, it would be fairly natural to ask the question "So if I am not the one doing it, what is?" Or if you are religious, of course, "Who is?"

This question most often leads the spiritual seeker to consider oneself as "being lived." And because the seeker is now being lived, it must also have divine intentions behind it. Perhaps it does. I honestly cannot say it does or does not. But if there is a divine intention, it must also include everyone and everything – yes, including those heinous individuals walking around, too, those people you really despise and all those yucky creatures you think are ugly or annoying like blood-sucking mosquitoes.

The big problem with the "I am being lived" idea that is so prolific in spiritual circles is that it is clearly bringing the "I" back in through the back door, just an I that is now not even a bit part player, more of a silent witness or spiritual voyeur who just has to take what's coming to it, smile and grimace as the turds come down the line, a partial existence; because the very notion that I have no say in anything is so galling and repugnant. This "I" object is trapped inside the mind unable to control or manage its life, but it has faith it will be alright on the night. The seekers conclusion is that the worse it gets the more I must be learning which is a good thing for me right?

This last paragraph is a typical way in which mindfulness is taught. It creates the illusion, or rather strengthens the illusion, that there is some entity here that is observing the proceedings in one's life from a nice safe distance. This might be useful as a temporary measure if there is trauma --- a kind of time out --- but ultimately, a full engagement with life will keep coming around again and again and often in even more demanding ways.

Here is a very typical example of the use of the word *mind* in the English language.

"I am troubled by my mind."

Surely, if you had control over an object called "the mind," you would put an immediate stop to its troubling behaviour. Put the brakes on those thoughts at 3 a.m. that appear to trouble that person who owns a mind.

"She pushed the thought from her mind."

A final example of how the word *mind* is used in the English language implies a user of the mind very much like we own a mind as a tool.

The physical presence of a possessed object called the mind is most often assumed simply because the thoughts that arise within it are different from the thoughts another person is having; plus, you cannot guess what I am thinking. Thus, logically then, *I* have a mind that is not *your* mind.

But as I discussed in Chapter 1, those thoughts are not *your* or *my* thoughts, they are merely random energies that arise. Thus, ownership of those thoughts happens after they have arrived. They are owned by a further thought called *me*. Is the process of thought-ing evidence enough for the ownership of a mind? What happens to the "my mind" claim when there are no thoughts at all?

Getting back to the question in hand about the location of the object you can hear outside. Is it inside the mind or outside the mind? Many people being asked this question would immediately say that the bird in this case was outside the mind, the bird is somewhere over there singing in that tree although I cannot see it. Clearly, the physical bird itself is not inside the mind, especially when you think the mind is inside your head...that would be rather uncomfortable.

The hearing mechanisms we call ears on the sides of our head are picking up soundwaves, which in turn are translated by the brain, and the mind says that is a bird. That is what we have been taught. This whole assumption that the bird is outside my head is because you believe the mind is inside your head, without the position of the mind being here where I am where is the bird in that apparent 3 dimensional space? In other words, there are two very distinct realities or worlds:

there is *me* "inside my mind" where I exist, then there is everything else -- which we call "outside of my head." Imagine if I said to you there was no difference at all, that inside and outside were one and the same. How might you react to that? What would that feel like to the tiny separate *I* in the mind in charge if it were exposed to such vast spaciousness?

Before I try to persuade you that this might be true, it would be reasonable for me to tell you a story about a meditation experience I had in 2016.

At some point back then, I read a line in the Buddhist canon of sutras called the Heart Sutra. The teaching that stands out that you may have read and quickly passed by reads as follows: "Form is emptiness and emptiness is form." When I read this, something in me did a "ping" --- or even more accurately a "boom." It was so contradictory that it made no sense at all, but something here needed to find out what the hell that meant.

The word *emptiness* to my Western mind-set meant nothing at all, zip, squat. So how can nothing be something. It took several books and many hours, in fact two straight years of contemplation and meditation on this contradiction, to start to get a handle on the Buddhist meaning of emptiness. But one day during a spring walk looking at daffodils, it finally dawned on me the complete inseparable nature of that flower within the landscape. Although it appears to us as separate from the soil, the grass, and sky around it, it clearly was not an independent object. The flower was not only entirely dependent on that environment, it was that environment, yet simultaneously and paradoxically not that environment.

The petals, leaves, and stems were made up of decaying matter that was once living organisms. It was made of the sun, moonlight, and rain, which in turn were once rivers and the sea; which in turn were once clouds, which were once humans and animals. It was impossible to see the origins of anything.

Later that evening, as was my habit back then, I sat down to do a meditation. At the time, I was still living in my mother's spare room, and so sitting meditation had to be timed with her bedtime and the noise of the public house or bar. So, I sat down to sit, window open as usual, to listen to those sounds and observe the subsequent annoyances and internal frustrations of living in a town instead of up a mountain as a monk (a monk with ensuite plasma screen and Waitrose supermarket nearby!).

A distant car was driving by. The sound grew louder and then without any warning, my body started to vibrate and shake --- the sound of the car was not outside. There was no such demarcation as outside or inside, the body was indistinguishable from the sound of the car or any other object in the room and, in fact, all objects were inseparable. There was no "my mind," either, there was just mind. It was clear that mind itself is not only not personal but also not a localised phenomenon at all. It was everything, yet not anything at the exact same time.

If the daffodil were able to communicate that this was its reality, how would it do so? It would not be impossible to do so without a point of reference for itself: Clearly, that point of reference in humans is the *I am* or sense of self, but it is no more than a temporary default position mostly interpreted and sustained through language. No wonder the greatest teaching of all is silence!

This experience, although brief, appeared to shift consciousness into a whole new lens on the world. The next day while driving my car, it was as if the oncoming cars, the very landscape around me was moving through me as opposed to my moving through it, like I was wearing a virtual reality headset. It made complete sense of what Hui-Neng, the Zen sixth patriarch, meant when he said to the two monks arguing about whether it was the flag moving or the wind moving: "It is neither, it is your mind that is moving."

This year, 2020, I was walking the dog, and again without warning --- although this time a whole lot less abrupt than the first time --- it happened again. Slowly, bit by bit, the whole physical landscape in front of me was no longer distinguishable between an outside and an inside of my mind. The clouds were moving through the mind, any thoughts that arose were entirely insignificant, equal to the trees and clouds within that panorama. I was merely an object within the mind, not *my* mind, just mind, because everything was the mind. This experience lasted for several hours. It was not frightening or in any way special, it was completely normal. I can imagine, though, that if this experience happened to a tightly contracted sense of self out of the blue, it might be mistaken for a nervous breakdown, as one cannot locate oneself within the vastness of the landscape.

If you had spoken to me about a drama you were having, it would have appeared as you standing and pointing at a leaf on the ground and screaming and shouting at me how utterly important that leaf was, stamping your feet and screaming, "Look, look at this!"

Although the intensity of this experience appeared to fade, it never completely went away. It cannot. Now when I meditate, this illusory veil between inside and outside that appears to be so convincing falls away in moments. Those birds singing, airliners, the wind in the trees, the entirety of what we think of as that stuff that makes up the world, is not outside or inside. The distinction simply does not arise.

Some further questions arise from experiences like these as they always do

What, for instance, happens to time if that physical space between objects disappears, dissolves? The apparent space between you and an object creates time: It takes time to walk from here to the kitchen. But if the kitchen, like any other apparent object, is the mind, then time itself is an illusion.

If the mind is everything and everything is the mind, then mind ceases to be an object with actual form. If the mind is an object, it must have height, depth, width, it has some positionality about it. In English translation books of Chinese zen texts such as the book by John Blofeld *On Transmission of the Mind*, the Chan monk Huang Po uses the word *mind*, as in *your* and *my* mind, and the word Mind with an upper case M, as the same thing. This might be somewhat confusing for the reader until one gets accustomed to the text. Huang Po clearly states that all there is is Mind. If you're reading this and seeing the word *mind* with a lower case m, as in "you" thinking everything is "your mind," that really does muddy the waters, at least until you understand there is no such thing as your or my mind; or for that matter, Mind.

A name given to the experience I have described here is often called satori, or in Japan, kensho. It is why those who have appeared to experience this cannot tell you how long it lasted. Indeed it is an irrelevant question, because there is no sense of self experiencing it. The individual cannot experience its own absence. The sense of self is a temporal illusion bound by the constraints of a time-oriented lens; and when this is happening, the sense of self is not so much absent as something with no independent existence. It cannot, therefore, ever be absent. If that residual identity is present, it is no more or less significant than a stick on the ground or a fly on the windowsill.

To the sense of self that is incessantly troubled by the comings and goings of life, this might sound rather wonderful. And ironically to the sense of self that is having a bloody great time, it might sound crappy if not damn right frightening. The idea of not existing, however, is only relevant to a sense of self that exists. If the spiritual seeker is heavily invested in seeking out these so-called spiritual aha moments as evidence of one's path or evolution of personal consciousness, they are much mistaken. I will say more on this in another chapter.

In our society, some people are tortured by their minds, being personally attacked by this illusion. Doctors and mental health authorities medicate this object they call the mind. And they are not medicating the mind, they are merely slowing the brain's ability to translate consciousness; it is like throwing a blanket over a hi-fi speaker. People may even think they lose their minds. An interesting idea, that losing what you never could possess is defined as madness in the modern world, when it was once seen as a deeply spiritual experience in the past. To lose one's mind is to gain the whole universe.

Huang Po, the Chinese Chan master, was once asked the difference between his higher mind and his lower mind. His answer was rather lovely: he said, "Where do you keep all these minds?"

At the very most, the mind can only ever be an idea, a concept. As an idea or object, it becomes a thing, and as a thing, it must therefore be able to be controlled, it must have a location, it can be affected in some way, improved, impoverished even, messed up, and gotten out of. All these assumptions are primarily based upon the mind's being inside the physical body, specifically the head. In Chinese and Eastern culture, the mind is not located in the head, its positioned in the same place as the heart. In the West, children when asked where it hurts will still point to their stomach area even if the pain is in the head.

In Chinese Zen or Chan, they have taken this one step further. If the mind is not yours or mine --- which must be quite clear by now --- then is there a mind at all? How can a "you" point to such a thing as the mind if there is no you to point to it? Is there any actual separate object here, let alone an object called the mind?

Makes you think, does it not?

Chapter 4

Feelings

'Don't destroy the emotions of people, only teach the cessation of thoughts'.

Xin Ming

Before I wrote this chapter, I realized a distinction needed to be made between emotions and feelings; also, however, to point out that in our language those two are often interchangeable. I might, for instance, be sitting in front of a fire and feeling warm, but that does not necessarily mean I am emotional about feeling warm; rather, that feeling warm might at some point make me emotional, especially if the warm becomes hot. You can see how the words can be somewhat tricky to use.

I asked the question long ago why I seemed to enjoy those feelings that were considered negative. Sadness, anxieties, internal stories of things that happened years before that I had wished had turned out differently but that still made me angry. I was a master at suffering due to emotions. I considered myself an emotional man who was in touch with his feelings. I was so in touch with them that I created a soundtrack to boost their effects on me. I must really have enjoyed them, milked them for all their worth. I would drive to a dreadful job, put on some Radiohead and get a full fix of misery; and by the time I arrived, the confirmation bias that my life and marriage sucked were complete.

It became clear once I was conscious of that habit that negative feelings in some way made me feel good about myself. Within that tight insular space of my mind and car, I could directly manage those feelings like some hypnotised orchestra conductor. Suffering via emotions through negative mental imagery of myself was my addiction. But why?

When the *I* is suffering, it is playing out the tragic character on its own stage, it is out there in the spotlight going for the Oscar-winning performance. If I am feeling this way, then I must be right about those events that happened in the past or are happening now. Being right must mean I exist. To continue to prove my existence, I must keep the habit going; and the most readily available drug is the potent suffering that I was capable of orchestrating. Competitive suffering with yourself makes one version of you right and another wrong, a higher virtuous character criticizing and putting down the other version of you that never gets anything right.

The beauty of negative feelings is that they not only embellish and expand our sense of well-being in the world, they make us feel safe as well. But something else is happening here. We hate negative feelings, we want to control them, reduce them because we are conditioned into believing that negative emotions are in some way dangerous to our continued existence. We fall into an endless cycle of expanding ourselves through seeking out stuff to suffer over, then try to control those things; which offers us an even greater illusion of control, thus offering us further evidence of our own existence.

So, there is this dreadful juxtaposition between the addiction to suffering and the seeking out of those things that make us suffer and the simultaneous desire to distance ourselves from those things. It is like the drug addict that needs a fix and at the same time is appalled by the dependence upon it.

So, to recap. We love to suffer and seek out new and interesting stories of suffering, perhaps television films, dramas, and especially the 24/7 news updates. And at the exact same time, we are trying to distance ourselves from it as well.

With the latter, I have coined a nice little phrase for this; I call it "self-distancing." Self-distancing is not only the energy we invest in distancing ourselves from those emotions but the insane habits we employ to do that.

There is a world of options available for helping the illusory mirage of the self to distance itself from itself, some of them seemingly sold as beneficial to the reluctant feeler. Look at what is on offer to reduce feelings we do not like. There are the soft drugs that mildly anesthetize the feelings. Popular ones include chocolate, cheese, cake, they all work well, or even a nice warm bath with a glass of wine, maybe a holiday to find the other version of "you" that you prefer.

Some have a spiritual edge to them. Often, meditation is sold to reduce stress and anxiety caused by unwanted emotions. Then the medium drugs: wine, beer, weed, coke, nicotine, sex are a few popular ones. If this does not work, try the hard stuff! Lowering the level of consciousness with heroin, pharmaceutical meds, or if you really cannot handle feelings at all, perhaps suicide and death, although there is as yet no evidence that death works. They are all about not feeling feelings that happen.

The question that has not yet been asked is "Was there ever a choice to not feel?" How can a person physically remove oneself from oneself? How on earth is a *you* going to distance itself from the you feeling?

Is that not the game we all play repeatedly?

This question rather implies, like the previous chapters, that there is someone here that can or cannot feel, as if there is an off-switch we have yet to discover. If the environment and all that includes are the primary source of thoughts and it is clear to us that we have little or no control over that, what of the subsequent emotional contractions and expansions caused by those. Do we make ourselves once again the perpetual victim without any control, or is there a possibility that there never was anyone here with control in the first place therefore a victim as well? We fall head long into the trap of believing that if we start from a position of control we will then lose that, what happens if we start from the position of never ever having control, what is it we can actually lose?

Let me offer an alternative option at the risk of falling into self help! Which I intend to do just for ease of explanation I will tell you what a meditation experience might be like.

Because we rely on thought and concepts as mapping structures to our sense of well-being, what would happen if we did not name an emotion? What would that look like and if it were possible, would this practice stop the cycle of needing to reduce or control feelings we do not like. In meditation practice particularly, I have practised this for several years, mostly out of personal curiosity. I might notice during the day that there is trapped energy that has a demanding element to it, it makes itself known much like a stone in your shoe would. I will sit down on my zafu cushion not to reduce this feeling or create imaginary distance but to feel it fully.

It's important that there be no subtle deals being made here when this is tried out. Try it out not because you want to reduce an emotion or make it go away, but simply because it's there and you're curious. What is the worst that can really happen?

In the silence of being, the feeling has no need to attempt to barge its way past the mind's control mechanisms. Most emotion spends time trying to get your attention, but we have been conditioned to keep pushing it away. Naming a feeling is about controlling it. When the feeling is not conceptualised, it has no added weight of history, it is free to expand outward throughout the body and then seemingly dissipate like a cloud on a summer's morning. We all have the tendency out of habit to push those unpleasant emotions down into the solar plexus area of our body where they fester and can even cause disease. Sometimes this practice helps stops the person being the victim to emotions, and perhaps even more than that, it's direct evidence that no one here will be killed or hurt by emotions. Imagine not being afraid of difficult emotions.

Naming an emotion is also about ownership. Because of the nature of language, as soon as something is objectified, it becomes "ours" or "theirs." I am angry, not there is anger happening.

Let me give you an example of an emotion with bad press, especially in spiritual circles.

Have you watched a wasp trapped at the window in the summer, buzzing up and down the glass? It looks angry, so we say, "be careful, this wasp is angry." The wasp is displaying signs that anger is happening, but we do not invite the insect to stop being angry by talking it through with us or suggest that it seek out therapy. We know instinctively that as soon as the wasp is released, its anger will naturally reduce. What we are seeing is anger displayed, not wasp plus anger.

The wasp lacks the self-awareness to know its emotion is anger because it does not continuously conceptualise its experience as personal; so it does not try to distance itself from itself. If we see someone as displaying anger, especially in spiritual circles, we make all sorts of assumptions that are entirely inaccurate.

If, however, the spiritual person displays only those emotions that we consider virtuous, we conclude that this person is awakened.

Are emotions ours? They certainly appear to happen to us because we display emotions that are not being displayed in another person. I might be crying with laughter at a black comedy whilst the person sitting next to me might be deeply troubled by the jokes. Personally, I do not think asserting that feelings and emotions are not ours has any merit. There is already a mass movement away from feeling feelings that we think are negative. Think about the pharmaceutical business that is mostly reliant on people not wanting to feel.

I think that, firstly, educating and learning the skilful means to fully experience emotions in all their colours would be far more beneficial to the seeker. There are way too many spiritual folks out there denying their experience through dissociation, pretending to be awakened. A truly awakened individual displays a full array of emotions without the need to judge them as good or bad. Like the wasp, it simply is what is happening.

Try to imagine not being held hostage by emotions and feelings, what would that be worth?

What we are being held hostage by is the thought that is describing the emotions, not the emotion itself. It is the continued on-going narrative that 'I' do not want to feel this, I only want to feel that. The only truth I can tell you with all honesty is that there was never a choice to start with. It would be perfectly normal to not like this very much, but you might find that in this statement there is a greater liberation than you can imagine.

<u>Chapter 5</u>

The Body

'To play hide and seek with myself is a game that even small children do not play'
Wei Wu Wei

The reason I left this chapter as the last card in my house of cards is simple. The body is a storehouse in which everything appears to happen. It is where we have been conditioned to think the thinker of thoughts occurs, it is where we are taught that the mind lives, it is the appearance of a person experiencing emotions and feelings. And all of this gives rise to the sense of self that is who and what we think we are.

The physical body is the most convincing evidence we have that there is an independent entity here that exists. Say to a Zen master, "I do not exist," and you will get your nose pulled or a stick across the back and asked the question "So if you do not exist, who is feeling the pain?" But more on this type of stuff in the "Enlightenment" chapter.

As we all have a body, it would be almost impossible to generalise about body stuff and simply say that *this is how it is*; it is bound to contradict your personal experience. You can imagine that writing a chapter called "Body" in a spiritual seeking—oriented book is a tough ask, trust me --- it is, I don't feel particularly qualified to do it justice. So, I am going to stick to my apparent personal experience and hope that I can bring some new and interesting insights.

I liken the physical body to a tuning fork, those extremely sensitive pieces of metal that musicians use to keep their instruments in tune. As a musician myself, I noticed that if I have a tuning fork in the room with me, it will vibrate to anything else that is vibrating in its own key, even from some distance.

The body, being the form in the Buddhist Heart Sutra but at the same time the emptiness that is that form, would appear as energy packets called quanta. On the quantum level of reality, it would be impossible to see you and the chair you're sitting on; you literally would be indistinguishable from the environment around you. In this quantum world, you would put your hand out to touch another object and there would be no such object touched by a *you*.

Look around you now: Are you in a city high-rise flat? A house full of electrical devices all switched on? Or perhaps if you are lucky enough, the more natural flow of energy of a park environment? Or better still, a forest. Try to visualise the different and often disruptive energies bombarding the physical body right now.

The body is a living antenna for an endless stream of information most of which is unconsciously received. This information will be translated as thought, feelings/emotions, physical sensations in the body --- and all apparently performed by this object called the mind. This, then, is the matrix that gives rise to the sense of self, which then lays claim to those functions as its doing. Because of this, the sense of self tries endlessly to control those things in order to preserve its own illusion as that which is in charge....in other words, a ceaseless cycle of chasing its own arse!

The self as temporal entity --- that is, a time-based illusion that exists in the past -- leads to a constant state of playing catch-up because those events it sees as dangerous to its continued existence have already occurred. The desire to control these events in the environment that appear not to be favourable to its continued survival are felt in the body as incessant doing. The more those events appear as threatening to the sense of self, the more action is required by the body. Look at the world, is it not full of selves all running around trying desperately to cling to some idea of control so they will not die! ...and in this process concurrently consuming the planet's resources.

This incessant doing carries on until the body is worn out and can no longer continue to keep up the charade of protecting this fictitious entity that thinks it is in charge. The body has its own intelligence, which through a war of attrition with this sense of self battles to keep itself in a peak state of health. Rarely does the sense of self give in; it forces the body to do crazy things like run marathons for egoic kudos, or worse still physically cut the body into weird shapes in order to fit the present understanding of beauty.

The body today exists in a constant state of psychological fear, primarily because we are being told by the media that we are under constant threat from something that will kill us. Imagine doing to a household pet or to a young child what the media is doing to the human body? It would be considered abuse, and you would most likely be heavily fined or sent to prison.

But the habit of continuous identification with thinking and thought is that it tells the body that events are happening now when clearly they are not. There might well be war somewhere in the world, but it's not happening in your lounge. Yet how can the body know the difference? If you have a lemon or an apple in the kitchen, go and look at it for 30 seconds; the body will have a physical response to the thought, hormones, enzymes, and chemicals that are being released into the brain.

Now head back into the lounge and switch the television on. Watch the news at the top of the hour about Covid-19 or perhaps a war kicking off somewhere, and see how it is interspersed with advert nasties about starving children and abused animals, or maybe the subliminal messaging for a great big cheese-covered pizza so you can feel better about those events. Incessant 24/7 stimulation with extraordinarily little downtime piped through your mobile phone keeps the body in a fight-or-flight response to events that are not happening to the body watching them. The media relies on a message that says, "Unless you know what is happening, you are in danger, SO PAY ATTENTION!"

How much of the time do we spend seeking out those things that make us suffer that are really about continued desire to prove our existence? Isn't it ironic that those things that we seek out that provide us with stress, anxiety, fear, and worry are actually physically affecting the body's immunity through the excessive production of cortisol and are probably shortening its life span. It is another example of our addiction to suffering.

Let me give you an example of the most recent event that happened to me that is further evidence of how the body reacts to emotions, even ones I thought I was conscious of.

Not so long ago, I visited my mother's house in Surrey in the United Kingdom. This was the house that I moved into postseparation and divorce. Apart from the huge generosity of my mother who was kind enough to put me up and help me get back on my feet, the house itself held a great deal of sadness for me, and memories, most of which I had hoped to have already uncovered, felt, and let go of.

But you can never tell how much of that stuff is still lurking. On this visit, due to circumstances out of my control (yes, I know, very funny), I didn't get to spend much time with my daughter whom I usually visit at the same time, and the time I did spend with her I spent in my ex-wife's house along with my new wife, Shelley.

I thought I was conscious of any mind demons, old habitual thoughtforms, and their consequent emotions. I had plenty of warning beforehand that this event was going to take place. It went perfectly well --- no dramas, and it was lovely to see my daughter, Fern.

However, the next morning as I was putting down the lightest of bags onto the bed, my back spasmed. A white light of shooting agony powered up one side of my spine, making me draw in a deep breath, momentarily standing still, too frightened to move an inch. This pain was deeply familiar to me and I immediately knew the body was responding to emotional energy bound up due to the visit, rather than anything physically taxing. I had, of course, visited my mother many times since leaving, and for that matter my ex-wife's house, too; and without this pain, but not these exact circumstances.

In the past, I would have also been caught up in an emotional rollercoaster of internal dialogue, the sense of self clambering up the walls of how and why this had happened, thoughts firing away like the Fifth of November, all trying to fix it. But being familiar with these old habits and patterns from the past, there was some space around the pain. The physical pain without the story appears like a lit match in a void of darkness -- nothing needs to be done accept to take some deep breaths and relax, become deeply conscious of the body's needs, which is not the same energy of what the self needs. The sense of self responds to physical pain like a child with a wasp in its bedroom: it tends to dramatize pain and make it all about itself, which of course is its default with everything.

Any unprocessed emotions can build up pressure like lava under the earth, and it will be felt as pain in the natural weak points of the body. Paying attention to the thoughts only fuels the emotion that will feed the body false information, which will increase the pain.

I have learnt through such series of events as these that the body responds to kindness and unconditional loving attention. Speak to the body like you would to a child waking in the night from a nightmare. As a parent, you do not burst into her room and admonish her for waking you up, you hold the child without any conditions. This is the same love you show the body. Be kind to it when it hurts! When it speaks, in its language of pain, it is communicating that something needs attention. In this circumstance, it needed more conscious awareness of the emotional energies being fuelled by old thought habits. The sense of self does not know how to do this. It can only do it through the lens of "What's in this for me?" Deal making is its raison d'être. "If I do yoga every day, then I will be healthier and live longer and be more awakened than that other person," or "If I stop eating crisps, I will be more attractive to what's his name in the office, which means I won't feel so lonely."

If the body's communications are ignored over a great deal of time, it can cause serious illness and chronic pains. In our society, it's traditional to just swallow a pill, which is a bit like putting fresh cream on a dog turd. Before popping pills, there are many other possibilities to look at first. I truly feel that repressed emotion and traumatic memory are the origins of nearly all disease.

It was crystal clear once more how the body is directly affected by the energy of thoughts and emotions, and in this case, those were of the end of my marriage and separation from my daughter. How many times have we avoided spending time with certain people because they physically drain us, or perhaps we want to spend time with someone special because we feel revitalised and charged afterwards. There are several people in my life, some of them even family with whom I will physically avoid spending too much time. The unconscious desire of their own sense of self to continuously want to put themselves at the forefront of every conversation is emotionally and psychically draining for me. I can only spend so much time with someone that keeps saying, "Look at me, look at me, I need attention." Playing parent to a sense of self that is utterly determined to keep suffering is not a great way to spend time, even though you may know there is no one suffering outside the idea of that happening. It is important that the act of self-compassion include your own needs as well, especially how the body is responding to that.

The physical body is not a piece of meat, as some spiritual teachers teach. It is the house in which the universe knows itself. To simply dismiss its importance here is to miss a direct avenue to what it is that the seeker desires the most, which is enlightenment. I noticed in my own apparent path that any unprocessed emotional trauma acts like an anchor to the awakening process. We keep getting pulled back again and again to an event or events that we simply do not wish to face, like being attached to an elastic band. We leave bits and pieces of ourselves all over the place, attaching great importance to maintaining the illusion that we were right about something, and the body is the library of those memories. It reminds us of them like a repeated call from the library about a book that was checked out long ago that needs returning.

Buddha understood this when he realised asceticism was not the path to enlightenment, that moment when the shepherd girl offered him some rice in milk and he saw that her compassion towards him and his emaciated body was a door to deeper understanding of himself. To be compassionate towards the body is the mustard seed that gives rise to compassion towards all of life. If it's difficult to be kind to your own body, how much harder will it be to show kindness towards anything else!

In Chan Buddhism or Chinese Zen, they teach that the body is an object in Mind -- Mind in this case being a pointer to the absolute. And during satori, that is most definitely the case. The body appears as no more or less important than a pebble on the ground. But as this is not most people's experiences from day to day, it is not that helpful to us.

So, as you may have worked out while reading this book, the general theme is a simple question. Is anything here yours?

Well, clearly, by now you might be questioning whether "your thoughts" are yours.

Do you own such an object called *the mind*? Are you in charge of feelings and emotions, are you in charge of the body? If you oversaw the body, it would be pain-free, probably slimmer, and attractive to every man and woman on earth, right?

In spiritual and religious narratives, the most common theme is that you are a soul or spirit that lives in the body, a kind of ghost in the machine idea. I really like this idea because it means I get to eat cheese and have sex in another lifetime (not at the same time, of course). But it does tend to lead straight back to being the victim imprisoned for the duration of a life span, unable to escape while I am being punished by physical pain and disease. That idea I really do not buy into at all.

This conditioning will also most likely lead to a reward and punishment strategy with the body: if I go for a nice long walk in the morning or head to the gym, that means because "I" have been good, I can go out on the piss this evening. If you are American, by the way, that means going out and getting drunk, not finding someone to make you angry, although that might happen too if you get drunk enough.

A body means there will be pain, physical disease, and decay; we look at a tree losing its leaves each autumn, but we do not weep and think the tree is in pain or for that matter dying. We tend to equate physical pain in the body as a prewarning of death, which is a very unhealthy viewpoint.

Pain is deeply unpleasant, chronic pain even more so. Living with daily pain is exhausting and can cause depression and make a person's life a living misery. It really does feel personal because it is not happening to someone else, it is happening to a *me*, which is what makes it feel personal; yet all of these chapters are asking, "who exactly is this *me*?'"

We rely on the premise that if I am feeling it, then I am also experiencing it, and such an argument is bloody convincing as well. What comes first, the pain or the experiencer of pain? Does pain need a person to exist? It clearly exists in those creatures we share the planet with, but a bird for instance does not own the pain as its own, it simply is pain. When we see a bird in pain, we project that the bird is experiencing pain rather than the actual reality that there is just pain and not a bird and pain. That is something that we would find almost impossible to conceive of through the lens of being a self.

The evidence that I am the experiencer is totally reliant upon the premise that there is an "I" here experiencing it. It would be more accurate to say that "there is pain happening" rather than "I am in pain." We seem absolutely determined to lay claim to everything that is happening here as if the words themselves are evidence enough. This, of course, will lead to further assumptions that it should not be happening to me, why is this happening to me, god damn, this is always happening to me!

Physical pain is a universal experience, there is not a living creature on this planet that does not have pain. But to those creatures without self-awareness, pain is not personal -- simply because they do not have the story of the *me* that it is happening to.

So, what is physical pain like without the sticky incessant story of "me." Well, it bloody hurts, there is a preference for it to sod off, go away, please stop --- as Buddha said, "All life avoids pain." Pain with a less sticky *me* story running the body also has a vast expanse of space around it, no internal narrative of unfairness involved. The *I* is not in pain. It quite literally *is* pain, much the same way anything else happens here. Laughter happens, hunger happens, smiling, crying, burping and farting, giggling, and thirst; yes, and swearing out loud when you hit your thumb with a hammer happens, too.

Physical pain does not get added to a linear storyline of *me* and *my life*. This is a quite different way of experiencing pain --- and life, for that matter.

Chapter 6

Death

'Where the so-called problem of "death" is concerned it would seem reasonable to start by enquiring "What is there to die?"

We Wu Wei

To address the concept of death, I want to use a handy metaphor that has been hanging around for a while; it pops up now and then, and as I am writing about the one subject we all definitely have in common, let me put it out there for you.

I want you to imagine a large pot of stew on the cooker – vegetarian (not that this matters, of course, but if you are one, which is probably likely as clearly only vegetarians reach enlightenment, it's best to stick with what works for you).

This pot of stew full of vegetables bubbling away on the stove is the absolute, it's the Self (uppercase S), it's Consciousness (uppercase letter C), it's the universe, it's *I Am*, it is whatever concept you really like that is the pointer used in spiritual texts typically called everything.

For this chapter, I will use the word *Absolute* as my pointer towards that which is everything all the time. The pot, which is the absolute, appears as infinite forms; it's bubbling away on gas mark 4, to extend the metaphor.

So, let us assume you are standing there watching this pot of the absolute mixed vegetables bubbling away. As you look at the surface of the pot, you see a pea rise to the surface. We could describe this pea as "being," or in our language "being born"; that is, it appears to have come into existence. When the pea vanishes from sight again, let me call this "nonbeing"; we call that nonexistence "death."

The apparent duration between the coming into existence (being) and the going out of existence (nonbeing) we call "time." Time is a measurement of that space between being and nonbeing. This space between apparently coming into view and then going out of view we call "our life" or simply "life." But you could extend this metaphor to pretty much everything in your life --- thoughts, sounds, sights, smells --- literally everything you think is your personal experience is simply the coming and going of appearances of objects without independent existence, much like the mirage in chapter 2. Spiritual seekers being timebound entities within the story of themselves often but rather mistakenly call this their path. Paths always lead from here to there, but as there is no here or there the path is somewhat a redundant fantasy, albeit a nice one.

But because the pot is always utterly full all the time and nothing can be added or taken away from it, it only appears that something is born, created, and then dies, is destroyed. But nothing at all has happened. Nothing has ever actually happened here – ever.

We cannot even say something was born and changes through that apparent lifetime; it completely negates the concept of impermanence, because the concept of impermanence is reliant on an object that has been born and changes. Or perhaps that is really all that is happening here? The pea appears to come into existence or, in our language, is born. It appears to stay a while, goes through changes creating the illusion we call time, then ceases to exist, which we call death. But what really happened? To the sense of self deeply entrenched within its own story of seeking absolution, awakening, enlightenment, and so forth, the very notion that nothing at all is happening here can only be received and rejected as nihilism. No self-respecting individual heavily invested in saving oneself will readily accept this, and ironically neither can this individual accept nor surrender to such ideas, as to accomplish that would require a self.

We cannot even say that there is a past, present, or future; because again that would mean that something was created, created in the past, existing in the present, dying in the future. Those people desperately trying to reach Eckhart Tolle's eternal land of the "now" are all destined to remain deeply frustrated because they themselves can only ever be the concept of the present in perpetuity. Any movement towards is always a movement away.

If we ask the question "What about the physical body, that surely dies!" Well, yes, in one sense that is true, it does appear that the body is born, lives, then dies. But that again is the illusion of the pea coming in and out of existence. All of those chemical elements that make up the physical body have always been here. When the body decays, those elements are recycled into something that we will call existence. Perhaps the water in the body will even become a river, then a cloud, then something that future generations will drink. Each glass of water you drink was someone or something.

What about the sense of self, is that alive? Well, each pea has certain characteristics that make it appear to be a unique object. But as the pot is everything all the time, that pea has always existed. It cannot cease to exist because it was never born. In the very same way, sense of self cannot cease to exist simply because that too never had any independent existence. As we discussed in Chapter 2, it's reliant upon the environment; and that environment is the pot of vegetables.

Can we know this pot of veggies I am calling the absolute? It cannot be known because what you *are* is it. In order to know it, a *you* would have to be separate from *it*, and you are not. Anything you call the Absolute or the Self is nothing more than an imagined object, a thought; and as we know, a thought is not the thing itself, it is a description of an object.

So, the concept of death, this idea that human beings are stalked by in all manner of dread, that thought of not existing at some point in an imagined future that drives the seeker to be enlightened, this is merely a made-up idea. Those people that we loved and now miss because we consider them to be dead are still here, they can never not be here. But like the pea in the pot that is no longer visible, we say they no longer exist...or in human language? They are dead.

The huge loss to the sense of self when someone we love physically dies is like a huge space opening on the ocean floor. The ground beneath its feet is pulled away and this sudden expanse of spaciousness that bursts into the story of me and my life is what we call "grief." On a smaller scale, there are endless mini-griefs that can be felt when perhaps we get fired or someone we're very much identified with has an affair. A small part of the story is altered then, and if this change is against the perceived will and control of the sense of self, it can feel equally devastating to that sense of self; a mini-death, in fact. These endless mini-deaths are common throughout the life of the sense of self.

Take retirement, for instance, the career identity that has been deeply invested in throughout the individual's life span. When that ends, all sorts of emotional upset, anxiety, and stress is felt, as that part of the story of the sense of self has been lost. Imagine the picture of a person's life as a jigsaw puzzle. The sense of self continuously tries to fit the bits together to make a tangible story of itself about which it can say, "That is me," but the bits keep floating off into space because of the illusion of impermanence; the edges of the *me* narrative keep getting eroded. It takes a great deal of effort to gather in all those bits of the jigsaw that make up the story, it is something that people spend every waking hour doing. But sometimes, often in fact, great big chunks of the jigsaw of the *me story* break away like coastal erosion after a great storm.

This space, or more accurately the emptiness, appears to barge its way between those bits of the jigsaw that make up the self. At first, this experience is most often defined as fear because the self has lost its cohesion and continuity, new identities and storylines must be sought out as soon as possible, and if not, then I am suffering. But this emptiness is what has been described as the grace of god or unconditional love. There is a certain irony to that as what we desire the most is that which we fear in equal measure.

The illusion of the death of the self is all that is required to know the grace of god, yet this isn't possible because the self was only ever the mirage drawing the dying man into the desert. The man known as Jesus went into the desert to meet his own illusory sense of self as the Devil. Siddhartha went into the forest to meet his own sense of self called Mara. And even why Muhammad went into the desert hermitage into a cave to receive the message of Allah. And since those sages, many thousands of men and women have followed the path of the deathless death.

But in the end, when all is said and done (and other similar classy cliches), no-thing ever came into existence so no-thing can ever cease to exist. Many people who have experienced a complete loss of self have come back afterwards and claimed to be god, once more objectifying that experience through the lens of the self, as only that can happen. Perhaps that is the sin of language and why so many sages such as Jesus have come to a rather sticky end.

Near to physical death, all those bits of the picture that make up each character in the story will float off into the void, revealing only this which was always here prior to that story's coming into play. This character we call Robin will appear as no more than a dream --- one of those night-time dreams we wake from that seem ever so convincing but which are relieved on waking only to discover it was a dream after all. All the worries, the fears, the desires, the being right, the seeking a way out of this, preferring that, loving this, hating that. All nothing but illusions attached to the character in the story, I was but a moment's thought of myself.

Chapter 7

Enlightenment

'If you practice MEANS of attaining Enlightenment for three myriad eons but without losing your belief in something really attainable, you will still be as many eons from your goal as there are grains of sand in the Ganges'

Huang Po

Buddha was heard to have said, "**I truly attained nothing from complete, unexcelled enlightenment.**" This is not what the spiritual seeker that has spent hundreds of pounds on retreats, books, and endless YouTube videos plus hours of meditation really wants to read. Seekers of enlightenment are driven by the idea that they themselves can bring about the experience of enlightenment: to be worthy of it, to gather sufficient knowledge, to practice what the ancients have done, to be utterly disciplined and determined. This will lead naturally to more suffering, as one believes that there is something one has not quite got or just one tiny piece of the jigsaw one has not understood.

Many moons ago, when I too read Buddha's statement for the first time it too would have caused me nothing but cognitive dissonance. What does Buddha mean he got nothing from enlightenment? that cannot be right! There is simply too much invested in this from my perspective to quit now, there must at least be a reduction in psychological fear, some bliss, some deeper insights into the nature of existence. Born out of frustration of these promises not being met will either inspire further deeper study and seeking or increase the desire to quit but quitting only deepens the illusion of the doer trying to quit. It can lead to a one foot in, one foot out story which is very common in seeking circles.

The thing about those insights and revelations, those moments we live for, is that they feed the sense of self's desire to believe that it is just that tiny bit closer to getting that piece of the jigsaw it needs. It is as if the accumulation of spiritual experiences adds divine interest to a celestial bank balance. This balance is just another story, a story that is, of course, entirely fabricated and wholly reliant on the concept of linear time. That is, that within the story of the sense of self, there is always tomorrow when I might finally get it. Whatever it is that the sense of self has not got yet or understood, it's reasonable to assume that a "knower" is required; and clearly, by now, you might have a suspicion that there isn't one.

Do not forget that Siddhartha Gautama left a huge palace full of the best creature comforts anyone could imagine. He was a prince in waiting in a highly respected Indian royal family who was going to inherent huge tracks of land and armies to do as he willed. Huge amounts of cash, jewels, sexy dancing girls, top-class education pupiled by incredibly wise men of the time. We assume his parents loved him, and apparently his wife was a looker. And to finally top it off, he even left his children. Now what kind of crazy man does all of this? If Siddhartha had all this and it still wasn't satisfactory, what chance have you got?

Was it really just that Siddhartha also suffered from a massive cognitive dissonance when he saw the dying, diseased, and ageing citizens of his father's kingdom that day, or was it something that stirs much, much deeper in all of us. We are told that his heart was moved when he watched the insects of the soil dying under a plough. We are told that this compassion that he felt moved him so much that he wanted to find a way out of that inevitable demise that awaits us all, not just for himself but for all life thereafter. What a guy!

But let us be brutally honest here: I did not seek enlightenment to save your arse, I did it to save my own. If I am being completely honest, the driving force behind seeking in me was not the elderly and the dying in the street let alone the creatures under my garden spade whilst digging up my virtuous diet of organic vegetables, it was far simpler than that. It was to stop suffering once and for all, and the cherry on the cake was that if I could reach enlightenment, I might not need to come back to this crazy place we call Earth and spend several more lifetimes with you lot. In fact, I would be much better than you because I would be enlightened, I might even write a few multimillion selling paperbacks and start a retreat in Portugal.

It became increasingly clear that the search for enlightenment was really all about me and the story of me as the perceived sufferer. The more I saw myself as that, the more energy was invested in seeking a way out of it.

I did not just wake up one morning and, bleary eyed over my cornflakes, decide to seek enlightenment, just as a drug addict does not go from being a healthy well-rounded individual to scoring class A drugs in dark alleyways for fun. The individual must come under a certain amount of pressure; things must happen in one's life for one to get to the point when one thinks, *I cannot do this anymore*. The events in a person's life over time erode the sense of self repeatedly until something inside snaps. Whether one seeks enlightenment or becomes an alcoholic is anyone's guess; it can go in any direction. In the story of the self, all eventualities are happening simultaneously; no one knows what will happen, but you can guarantee something will.

It might not just happen the one time, either. The sense of self appears to have limitless energy for repeatedly rebuilding the house of cards; and each time, the structure looks a little bit more dysfunctional than before. But it always has an inherent weakness, so it will not be long before the house of cards --- that is, the story of me and my life --- starts to crumble again. The beautiful paradox with seeking enlightenment is that the seeker is not so much building up one's story with material wealth but in spiritual credits. But wait, is there any difference? Only within the story of *me* and my life, sure there is.

I am not going to go into personal stories of how and why I ended up seeking enlightenment, but I can guarantee that it is not a story of fairies and woodland nymphs spreading joy and peace. It is generally a war of attrition where the sense of self becomes an endless victim of itself. Only then does the seeker get to fecundity to find a way out from those events. So, for us in the 21st century, we are not leaving behind wealth and pleasure, peace and love, to seek enlightenment. We must start by admitting to ourselves that it is about not wanting to suffer anymore. Without suffering there is no seeking. I think that is why Buddha's story stands the test of time, because his story like all stories of suffering are universally the same throughout the ages.

The first thing we must do is admit to ourselves that we are indeed suffering. Suffering is not a word that is thrown around a lot outside spiritual circles and Buddhist-flavoured writings. The Buddha called it "Duhkha." Duhkha is not having your nails pulled or root canal work every week for a month, it is more accurate to describe the word as a sense of unsatisfactoriness. A background sense that something in your life just does not feel right, an agitation about life that you cannot quite put your finger on.

When these moments of consternation about our lives and the events in it come together more often than the happy ones, we might just say to ourselves, "I am suffering." For me personally, I see suffering pretty much everywhere all of the time, mostly because all I see is people chasing their arse desperately trying to control stuff that they think they need to make them happy. There seems to be a great virtue these days in having minute control over every aspect of our lives; we know how the rabbit got into the hat and how the magician pulled it out! Because if we know how that happens, it offers us the illusion of safety.

Enlightenment is the ultimate safety. If I am enlightened, there will be no more fear, and I will never ever need to feel frightened ever again. On a day-to-day basis, most of us are lucky enough to not have our lives threatened. Our physical body gets unwell from time to time, we might very occasionally fall out with our family and friends, but not so much that we should fear for our lives.

Far and away the greatest and most common fear is psychological fear --- that idea of ourselves in the mind that sees threats where there are none, the story of *me* and *my life* being nothing more than consecutive thoughts building up a story that needs constant fine-tuning. If I am not in control, the sense of self will feel fear. And feeling fear is the big no-no!

The fragmented story of the sense of self and its fear-based thoughts is the driving force behind seeking enlightenment. We might not like to admit this to ourselves, but if you are truly honest, it is that.

So, if there is no independent sense of self, how on earth can anyone reach enlightenment?

If I bring you back to the Buddha's words at the very beginning of this chapter " –**I truly attained nothing**" -- I think the clue was there from the onset. I believe Buddha didn't so much teach us how to reach enlightenment as that he actually kept asking us, "Who or what is it that seeks enlightenment?" It must have been thoroughly frustrating for him to teach people about how to reach enlightenment yet always know that this could not happen because there is no "I" there in the first place that could ever achieve such a thing.

I think that when it is said that Buddha taught people for 40 years but not a word ever ushered from his lips, it was a bit too subtle for most. It simply meant that although the Buddha spoke and taught, there is no man called *the Buddha* that ever said a single word, and no person ever heard such a teaching.

So, what might an enlightened person's experience be of the world. Well, as I am not enlightened, I will have to plagiarise my view on this by using a real-world example that occurred to me in hindsight.

About 3 months ago, I decided not to watch the mainstream news reporting of the so-called Covid-19 hysteria. I did this simply because I noticed that there was an addictive quality in needing to know what was happening. A perfectly sound reasoning towards what did look like some dreadful pandemic that was going to wipe out humanity.

By watching the TV news, I was thinking this is real.

By not watching the TV news, I was still making it real.

But through the lens of the enlightened, nothing at all is happening here.

Yes, I know! Wait -- let me put this another way, as that does not really make much sense.

When you go to sleep at night and you dream of monsters and dinosaurs or hot sexy sex with a fantasy woman or man, the dream you are having appears as being very real. But on waking up, you are endlessly thankful that you do not talk in your sleep; and your excuse, if you did say someone else's name in your dreams, is that you are not in control of your dreams.

So, was the dream real or unreal --- perhaps both at the exact same time. Do you see my dilemma here? To say that you did have sex with someone when you were dreaming is to make it real, to say that you did not have sex in your dream is also to make it real too.

We cannot say enlightenment does not happen, because that implies that it did not happen to someone. We cannot say enlightenment does happen because that implies it happened to someone. So, all we are left with is silence.

The silence of no words, no thoughts, no speech, no concepts.

This is as close as we can ever get. And even that is saying too much, because enlightenment is never close or far away.

As Huang Po was once heard to have said,

"Even if you go through all the stages of a Bodhisattva's progress towards Buddhahood, one by one; when at last in a single flash, you attain to full realisation. You will only be realising the Buddha-Nature which has been with you all the time; and by all the fore-going stages you will have added to it nothing at all. You will come to look upon those aeons of work and achievement as no better than unreal actions performed in a dream. That is why the Buddha said 'I truly attained nothing from complete, unexcelled Enlightenment.'"

Chapter 7

So, who gets saved?

'There are no sentient beings to be delivered'
Diamond Sutra

If we think about our moment to moment actions throughout any one day, is it not really all about building up and enhancing that sense of self that we identify as. It is as if we are a person sitting behind a machine incessantly turning knobs and making fine adjustments to a *me* for it to survive, actions of which we are mostly unconscious.

We have become so hypnotised by the thought of the *me* and its story that all our actions and words are hell-bent on protecting that. If we are not projecting those neuroses and fragilities of that *self* onto others, blaming them for that suffering, we think we are being tortured by personal thoughts in an object we call our mind.

We rarely ever stop long enough to really question what it is that is trying to save itself and from what exactly.

We all want a happy dream, we do not want to suffer, we want to be healthy, to live a fully contented life. If the sense of self manages to give itself a good life, it is called a life well-spent. That is like working and paying bills for the captain of a ship you have never actually met because we believe that if we do this, he will save us from dying when the ship finally goes down. It is nuts!

At the present time of writing, there are 7.8 billion people on this planet. Of those 7.8 billion, 6.2 billion believe in a god that will save them after they have died. Or another way of saying this is that 6.2 billion people think life will really begin to improve once they are dead. This cannot be a sane way to go through life. Look at our desire to save ourselves, yet not even answer the simplest of questions: "Where is this self?" that we are so desperate to save.

If you are at all identified as a separate individual on an apparent spiritual path believing that events are personal to *you*, then those events will have meaning because they appear to be happening to that *self*. The self will think that those events occur specifically for it to learn lessons in order to be worthy of awakening or enlightenment. This is nothing more than a self-serving confirmation bias without any ending because the self is time itself...watch a dog chasing its tail.

Are you old enough to remember those old fairground video games of driving a car through the night trying to dodge and avoid oncoming traffic? As a child, you held the steering wheel and diverted the car on the screen as the oncoming cars came towards you. This is really the perfect metaphor for the sense of self seeking to save itself. As it seeks, what it finds changes what is doing the seeking. This is the eternal illusion of a fictitious entity that thinks it is learning. As it learns and steers its way through spiritual lessons, it believes that it is moving towards fulfilment or absolution of some kind. But it is entirely stationary, stationary as the car on the video screen.

I do wish it were different, though. Like yourself the reader, it would be a beautiful thing for that sense of self to be worthy of a god it invented to judge itself by.

So, what next?

Well, nothing is next...apart from one small piece of information I thought I would leave to the very end just in case you had not worked it out yet. And that is that the sense of self never ever did a single thing ever, it has no desires, it makes no decisions, it has never made a single choice, it merely claims all of that.

So, who gets saved?

No one does. There is no one here to be saved and nothing to be saved from simply because there was never anything that was bound.

So at this point, you are either laughing or crying, or maybe both at once.

Chapter 9

A Conversation With a Famous Teacher

'Very truly I tell you son, the Son can do nothing by himself, he can do only what he sees his Father doing, because whatever the Father does the Son also does''

Jesus.

R: Hi! How are you doing, it has been a while.

J: I am really well, thank you for asking.

R: What would you like me to call you?

J: Just call me J, I prefer that to the messiah!

R: I can see that, quite a lot of pressure in being a saviour of one person, let alone a whole planet of people. So, can I ask you just one thing. What on earth were you thinking trying to teach super-strict Rabbis and Pharisees -- that there was "no god and you," that there was just this?

J: Haha – well, I was not the one thinking, clearly. I did try to say it in other ways such as "look under a stone and you will find me there"; but nobody said it quite so plainly as Francis, do you remember him? He used to do some teaching with Andrew…I think they are both saints now? He said, "Make me an instrument of thy peace"?

R: Francis, yes, I know him, lives down the road from me. I thought he had gone into retirement, but apparently he's still being an instrument.

J: Well, what he said really does point to what was going on for me at the time. It was like I suddenly found myself standing there in this temple in Jerusalem saying all this stuff to those Rabbis and I could not stop myself. The next thing I remember after what appeared to be an infinitely long pause of stillness was that they all went nuts and started to scream, bellow, and shout, some of them even threatening me with violence. I can tell you this: That day, I nearly decided to keep my mouth shut; I realised for the first time since coming out of the desert that what I was saying could get me into deep trouble; that people are just not ready to give up their beliefs, especially if they are the kind of beliefs that get to save them.

R: Are not all beliefs just deeply entrenched thoughts rooted in saving ourselves from some imaginary nonexistence?

J: Yes, that is true, but some are more pernicious than others, such as when a belief hypnotises a person and starts to take over one's actions and even kills other people because it feels threatened. This is what I meant by the word *sin*. To sin is to not see me, you see a belief of me or a thought of me instead, and I am never that.

R: Tell me about your trip to the desert.

J: At that time, I was suffering from dreams about not being able to find myself in this vast spacious darkness. I would sit in my room and look around me feeling woozy, staring at furniture, unable to make sense of where I began and the world around me ended. I tried talking to my mother, but she simply smiled and said, "Have faith, son." So, I packed some water and food thinking I would follow the caravan across the desert and go find myself.

R: Go on, what happened?

J: Well, I did spend a few days with some Bedouin; and then one morning, I woke up and they had left in the night. I can remember the previous night chatting with them around the fire about being one with the father and telling them stories of the three sons; and they did look at me like I was another crazy Jewish prophet, so I do not blame them for leaving. Anyway, I found myself in the desert, miles from anywhere with a couple of dates and a mouthful of water.

R: Sounds rough, what did you do?

J: Well, I picked myself up and started to follow the camel hoof prints in the sand, but that didn't last long once the wind came up; so I simply sat down hoping some other travellers used this route. After a couple of nights, I was starting to get really worried; I was dying of thirst and very hungry. I could hear voices on the breeze and see the universe in a single grain of sand. That was when it happened.

R: What happened?

J: You know, the thing.

R: What thing?

J: That moment I know you have also experienced, that singular moment when time ceases, when there is no *you* and the environment around you, when all is one, yet there is no one, there is just this, but there is no this, no nothing, yet it is everything all at once. It was for me at the time *god*, but that was the only language I had to make sense of it at the time. Eventually, some folks did come along and found me crawling in the sand dying of thirst. They looked after me for a few weeks; turned out I had been missing for about 40 days and nights. That was odd, because to me it felt like it had only been a couple of days.

R: And that was when you decided to head into Bethlehem and tell the pharisees that you and god were one.

J: Well sort of. I did not just get up one morning and decide to make my life much harder, to be followed about by lots of people suffering and in pain, that sort of just happened. As much as I tried to tell them that there was no one here suffering, the worse it got. I had to keep moving from one town to the next as if I were being lived, being driven by some unseen force to speak and share in the good news, to try and make sense of the experience I had had. I did not believe it myself; so, the more people I shared it with, the more real it became.

R: I know exactly what you mean, there does not seem to be a common frame of reference for it. It's as if you must create a new life for yourself, the *you* here that knows there is no "you" here, yet functions in a world that demands you play your part.

J: By the time of the Passover, I had quite a following, and the Romans were starting to take notice. The problem was that they had to keep an eye out for any uprisings; there were always groups of people trying to get the Romans to leave by causing trouble, and apparently, I had caught the eye of the governor.

R: I always wanted to ask you about that rich man and camel psalm you talked about. What exactly did you mean by that?

J: Well at the time, I had to teach in the language and convention that they understood. What I meant was that I was not talking about a rich man from the point of view of being materially wealthy, you know, having lots of gold. I was talking about a richness of knowledge, to gather spiritual information. The larger the ego and the more spiritual know-how you have, the further you are away from heaven ---

R: Heaven?

J: Yes, heaven. It's a word I use that points to this [he points to something just beyond his outstretched finger and smiles deeply].

R: Was it true that you met the Devil in the desert, and he tempted you three times?

J: No, that was not the Devil, that was me, that was my ego, those shadow parts of myself that I had been hiding from all my life. I came face to face with the fragility of myself, that sense of self that we judge as being less than better. By the time I was finished, all I could do was offer myself unconditional love and acceptance, which I know is insanely paradoxical, but there it is. At that point, all there was left was just me. The judgement completely stopped, and I was whole and complete. It was not that I was not whole and complete before, I simply stopped having conversations with an imaginary version of me in my head. The thoughts of inadequacy ceased --- it was just mental noise.

R: Is this what you meant about removing the branch from your own eye before removing the stick from mine?

J: No, that was something else. When I said, "Let those without sin cast the first stone," that was about our continuous self-judgement, that somehow god made us incomplete and that we are sinners. We project this lack of self-love for ourselves onto others and we judge them as we judge ourselves. Unless you love those parts of yourself that you hide from, how on earth can you show another any love and compassion. I realised that this was really what all of god's teachings were saying. It was never about ritual or making favour to a father in the sky --- what we had all been taught from birth --- all of that was simply a hidden exercise for self-compassion towards ourselves. The drinking of wine, breaking of bread, the reading of spiritual texts, community shared experiences, they are all disguised acts of self-kindness, a union of oneness. Treat others as you would have them treat you. It's pretty simple stuff.

R: That is a nice way of putting it.

J: Thank you, I still have a few nice ideas occasionally, except that now I know they are not mine [laughing].

R: So, what happened in the end, then, how on earth did you find yourself being crucified?

J: What?

R: History recalls that you were crucified by the Romans and spent three days on the cross and were then taken up into heaven. They call it the Resurrection --- the whole basis of Christianity is rooted in that.

J: Well firstly, let me put the record straight. I was not crucified at all. And secondly, what is Christianity?

R: Hang on! So, you were not crucified on the cross?

J: No, I certainly was not, I may have been arrested and questioned but I would remember being nailed to a cross, wouldn't I?

R: I am pleased to hear that. And the other thing, you mean you have never heard of Christianity?

J: No, what is that?

R: Well, that might take a while to explain [laughing]. But simply put, it's a set of beliefs that if you become more like you, then you too will have eternal life and live in god's house in heaven.

J: Are you telling me that after I left, they built a whole belief system out of the words that I said to them? Surely you're joking.

R: No, I am definitely not joking. Your simple message of self-compassion and treating each other with respect and kindness was turned into an act of virtue that later became very violent. Men put themselves above all other life and judged others as being less than virtuous, and some even tortured others who were clearly just being themselves and not Christ-like enough. They built massive temples to you and practiced being more like you once a week. You set the bar pretty high...so high, in fact, that the continued failure to be like you actually just creates the very suffering you intended to relieve them from.

J: Don't tell me anything more, that makes me deeply sad.

R: So what exactly did happen?

J: Well, we could see that the message I was speaking was actually starting to make people afraid and fearful; and when that happened, the crowd started turning nasty, so I and few of my friends hitched up to some traders and left for a place called India. At the time, spice traders were heading East so we worked our passage to the Indus. They said that there I would study Advaita texts and be amongst people that understood my experiences and would make sense of what happened in the desert. I spent the rest of my life there studying and meditating. I married a beautiful woman and had three children.

R: I think it was when you said, "I am the way and the light," it moved you from being a man and a teacher to a signpost to eternal life.

J: I never said I am the way and the light! I said "I am *is* the way and the light."

R: What is the way?

J: It's not an actual *way*, it simply means living your life not clouded by concepts and thoughts. When this happens, you are the seeing, the hearing, the functioning of spontaneous life. When I said I want you to have the fullness of life, this is what I meant. We miss the entire universe and all its beauty when we reduce it down to a thought. But I suppose that can be forgiven, as time does tend to shift meaning. I can well believe you about making me a saviour. The problem is that all the teachings can only be filtered through the sense of self, and as soon as that happens, it does the complete opposite --- it brings out the egoic need for power over others, the idea of one person being awakened and another not being. I suppose in the end, you need to experience it for yourself. Looking back, I was arrogant to think that I could teach that to those people. It was hot, dusty, and we were mostly hungry and not too happy. But as you yourself know, it's not your choice, it's simply something that is happening or not happening. It's of no significance to anyone in the end, is it.

R: I have some lovely Chinese green tea from the Mountains of Huang Po, would you like a cup?

J: I would love one! He's a great guy, you know.

R: Who is?

J: Huang Po, that big Chinese guy. He has a wicked sense of humour.

R: So I have heard. I found his book amazing, but each to his own, eh? [smiling]

J: Got any biscuits?

R: Yes, I will get some.

Printed in Great Britain
by Amazon